Christmas 2021

The Meaning Of Life
©Copyright 2023 Dave Williams, The Meaning Of Life

Dave
xxx

ALL RIGHTS RESERVED

No part of this publication may be reproduced, stored in a retrieval system, or transmitted, in any form or by any means, electronic, mechanical, photocopying, recording or otherwise, without the express written permission of the author.

Independently Published Totally Insane Project
ISBN: 9798-393884628

iDaveWilliams.com
@idavewilliams

The Meaning Of Life

Global Learnings Of A Travel Photographer

By

Dave Williams

CONTENTS

About the Author v

Why? vii

Fernweh 1

Ubuntu 15

Þetta Reddast 22

Sisu 29

Hiraeth 44

Samba 62

Keyif 70

Serendipity 77

The Call Of The Wild 89

Fjaka 100

Flâneur 107

muohta 113

SKÖP 121

No Worries 131

Níłch'i 137

Bifröst 149

Hygge 158

Coddiwomple 164

Resfeber 172

ABOUT THE AUTHOR

Hi team, I'm Dave Williams, a travel photographer, writer, and educator passionate about capturing the beauty of many destinations but emphasising Arctic locations through photography. My expertise in the northern lights is unparalleled. I'm proud to have written the best-selling book, The Complete Aurora Guide for Travellers and Photographers, which has received critical acclaim from photographers and travellers worldwide.

Throughout my career, I've been fortunate enough to deliver presentations and workshops on photography to audiences of all sizes. I'm honoured to be a member of the Photoshop World Instructor Dream Team, a select group of expert photographers and educators who share their knowledge and expertise with other photographers.

I've also had the pleasure of speaking at prestigious photography events such as Russell Browns Art Directors Invitational Masterclass, The Photography Show, including the Masterclass Theatre, as well as many online events and local camera clubs. My passion for finding unique perspectives in familiar locations is showcased in another book, The Eiffel Tower Effect, which has been highly sought after. My photo and collaboration clients include Adobe, NatGeo, Time, Forbes, Triumph, The Times, Passion Passport, KelbyOne, N-Photo, Lonely Planet, Expert Photography, and various airlines and media and travel companies.

As an aurora expert, I have an intimate knowledge of terrestrial and space weather systems and the Arctic landscape. This knowledge has been acquired by conducting a lot of research, leading me to discover many other exciting pieces of information throughout my journey.

My commitment to photography education and my extensive knowledge of Arctic locations and weather systems make me a noted travel photographer and educator. In my travel throughout the world, the concept I follow is 'once in a lifetime as often as you can.' My aim with this book is to encourage you to take opportunities to travel and have adventures and see the good in the world. I'm honoured to guide you on this exciting global adventure through lexicography and share my passion for travel with you.

Dave Williams
Photographer and Traveller

WHY?

I remember the night like it was yesterday. As a police officer, I had been trained to deal with difficult situations, but this was beyond anything I had ever encountered. We began a late turn at 1400 in central London, and it started just like any other. Rumours began to make the rounds that something was happening in Tottenham. The police station had been attacked, and officers there couldn't contain everything happening. It didn't take long for a group of us to come together and decide we were going to help. Driving a Vauxhall Astra with five big male police officers in full riot gear on blue lights and sirens was no easy task. Still, I managed to get us to another station, where we met with the other half of our crew and made our way north. After a confusing approach into the area and a rapid reverse manoeuvre that got us out of an ambush, I was on Tottenham High Road, clad in my riot gear, pushing back against a sea of angry protestors. They were hurling bricks, bottles, and anything else they could get their hands on at us, and we were doing our best to hold the line. The building next to us was on fire, the flames licking at the night sky. The intense heat made breathing in the thick smoke that filled the air even more challenging. We were trying to keep the protestors away from the burning building, knowing they could be injured or worse if they got too close. It turned out to be a carpet shop, which explained the many people we saw walking with carpet rolls over their shoulders as we entered the seat of the riot. We were severely outnumbered. We didn't have enough people to make a full serial (22), and the protestors knew it. Our weakness emboldened them, and they kept coming at us, wave after wave. We were doing our best to hold them back, but it felt like we were fighting a losing battle. Some approached alone and some in groups, some even in cars, driving straight at us before veering away at the very last moment.

Throughout the night, we were attacked from all sides. The protestors were determined to break through our lines and wreak havoc in the streets. We had to be careful not to use too much force, but at the same time, we couldn't let them get the upper hand. We felt our lives were at risk. This was ratified when we heard communications on our barely audible radios that a small group had broken into a nearby building site and attempted to hot-wire a JCB. It would undoubtedly have been our end if they succeeded, but we couldn't prevent it – our thin blue line was already stretched. If the whole scenario didn't already feel like a video game, it did the moment the police helicopter dropped low as an apparent show of strength to those in the building site, causing them to abandon their efforts and run.

As the night wore on, we grew more and more exhausted. Our arms ached from pushing back against the protestors and clearing the fences, palettes and other 'ordnance' they hurled our way. Our throats were raw from shouting commands. But we couldn't let up. We had a duty to protect the people and property of Tottenham, and we weren't going to back down. Little did we know we'd spend the following ten days and nights protecting the whole of London, and I'd end up being hit by a car in Greenwich, amongst many other things.

When the sun finally rose on the smouldering ruins of Tottenham, we were battered and bruised, but we had held the line. It was a small victory in the face of so much destruction, but it was a victory, nonetheless. At about 0900, 22 hours after we started that shift, we were replaced by officers from across the country who had received warning calls overnight – the entirety of the resources in London had simply been exhausted. As I removed my helmet and looked around at the devastation, I couldn't help but wonder what had led to the sheer scale of the destruction. Why had so many people taken to the streets in anger and frustration? Was there anything we could have done differently to prevent this from happening? I knew the story, of course. The reason the riots began was in national news headlines – the police had shot a member of this community. Allowing justice to take its course is one thing, but destroying your own backyard is quite another.

The Tottenham riots were a wake-up call for all of us. As police officers, we had to be better prepared for these kinds of situations and work harder to build trust and understanding with the communities we serve. It was a difficult lesson that we all took to heart. More than one year following the events of that night, I found myself in Simpson Hall at the now-sold and redeveloped Peel Centre – the training school of the Metropolitan Police. Myself and the rest of the serial who held our ground and contained the fury of the rioters that night received Commissioners Commendations with the following wording: -

For Bravery, Professionalism, and Dedication to Duty whilst under Serious and Sustained Attack for a Significant Period during the disorder in Tottenham on 6th August 2011

My police service lasted 14 years, and my photography hobby developed throughout. I was going to work on the streets of London, fuelling my thirst for photography and travel on my days off. My life at work as a police officer was packed with action and excitement. It was gratifying to help people in need while simultaneously bringing justice to those on the wrong side of the law. Still, over time with many negative influences from governments who were only looking to line their own pockets, things changed for me. I'd done the high-speed driving, I'd smashed doors down to find those evading justice, I'd been a public order commander, and it was time to address what was going on inside my heart. My photography grew and grew until it reached a tipping point, and I had to make a critical decision. Do I stay and live my life on the secure salary provided with far less job satisfaction than I'd previously had, or do I jump and carve my own path? If not now, when? There's never really a good time for such a monumental decision, and if I didn't just get on and do it, it would never happen. This dream of mine wasn't going to happen by itself. The objective was that of exploring the world, just me and my camera on a mission. I'd often said, 'Lend me your eyes, and I'll show you what I see.' This is something that I strongly feel we do as photographers — we show the world through our eyes. This dream was in motion, and let me tell you, without a doubt, the best dreams happen when we're awake.

Life is short, and the world is wide

The world is a vast and exciting place, rich in variety and potential. I'd nearly filled a passport with stamps on my rest days, but my brain's left and right sides were playing a severe tug of war. The stress didn't come from the decision itself. I always knew what the decision was going to be. The pressure came from constructing a mechanism to allow this dream to materialise and my life to change to one of adventure and exploration. The decision was made, and the adventure was underway.

As a professional photographer who travels the world, I have seen some of the world's most magnificent landscapes, from the vast African savannas to the snow-capped peaks of the Alps. But more than that, I've learned some of the most important lessons about love, life, and the human condition on my travels. I've created some pretty unique philosophies based on my diverse life experiences. I've often been asked, "Why don't you write a book about all this stuff?" Well, here's that book. We learn from life experiences. They translate into our everyday life. We should take every opportunity presented to us. We should do 'once in a lifetime' as often as possible. There are many phrases, sayings and words that have virtually no meaning. Take the age-old adage, "Never judge a book by its cover." This is simply irrelevant – it doesn't guarantee to be correct. We always judge things on first impressions, no matter how hard we try. While the saying "never judge a book by its cover" carries good meaning and is often used to encourage people to look beyond external appearances, it is not always relevant in practice. Humans often make snap judgments based on physical appearance or first impressions, whether consciously or subconsciously.

This tendency to judge others based on appearance is deeply ingrained in human behaviour and linked to our innate survival instincts. For example, we are wired to be more cautious around people who look physically imposing or aggressive. Similarly, we tend to be more trusting of individuals who present themselves as neat and clean. Furthermore, societal and cultural norms often reinforce this tendency to judge people by their outward appearance. In many contexts, appearance is seen as an indicator of success, social status, or even morality. For example, a person dressed in formal attire is often perceived as more competent and trustworthy than someone dressed casually.

Overall, while the saying "never judge a book by its cover" has some merit as an ideal, it is not always a practical or reliable guide for human behaviour. We should strive to be aware of our biases and look beyond appearances when possible. Still, we should also recognise that appearance can significantly impact how we perceive and interact with others. There are so many of these sayings that mean nothing. Still, globally, so many others have a translation deeply rooted within our psyche. I've gathered a collection of them on my travels.

The purpose of this book is to impart those teachings to you. I've interwoven life lessons and stories from my travels throughout each chapter. These notes are not intended to replace your own life experiences. In fact, I encourage each of you to explore the world and take your own version of this reality to form your own philosophies. There are humorous tales here, heartfelt ones, and outlandish ones. However, they have all made an indelible impression on me, and I wish the same for you.

The inspiration for this book came to me while I was enjoying a cappuccino and people-watching in a cafe in Paris many years ago. The variety of people's attire, hairstyles, languages, and habits stunned me. Despite our differences, we all yearn for a sense of direction in life. I've witnessed joy and sorrow in the exact moment as people celebrated and mourned. I've noticed that everyone is in a hurry, preoccupied with their jobs, relationships, and dreams, and often oblivious to their surroundings. The more I learn about the world, the more I understand that we are all on a journey of discovery, trying to make sense of this beautiful chaos. I resolved to begin penning this book. It was time to impart some of the wisdom I'd gleaned from my interactions with others, travels, and trials. I aimed to capture the spirit of my journeys and provide direction to those who might be lost. These stories come from my memory, travel notes, and a wealth of images that carry my mind's eye back to a place and time in my journey, often with an accompanying soundtrack! I'm often told how lucky I am to have this portfolio of images and experiences, but to that, I have just one thing to say: -

Luck is what happens when preparation meets opportunity

If we want to be lucky, the formula is quite simple. Be ready for the opportunity to present itself. When that opportunity comes along, no matter how long it may take, we'll be prepared and, therefore, lucky.

This book is neither a how-to manual nor a travel guide. It's a compilation of tales encouraging you to live a little closer to the edge. After all, if you're not living on the edge, you're taking up too much space. Each section provides insight into a culture and way of life. Love, death, excitement, and calm find their places in specific chapters. In common, however, is their insight into what it is to be alive and what it takes to live fully. It comes from inside my mind, but that is good for both you and me because we spend most of our time inside our own minds, so we need to make our minds the best place to be.

You'll meet some fascinating people on your travels, like the South African naturalist who taught me to be still, the Navajo woman who taught me the value of forgiveness, and the Norwegian fisherman who showed me the beauty of simplicity. From the arid landscapes of Morocco to the icy peaks of the Icelandic Westfjords, you'll read stories from some of the world's most spectacular sights. And you'll pick up some of the best advice I've ever received, like being okay with ambiguity, developing an attitude of gratitude, and savouring the present moment.

But the most significant takeaway, the thread that connects all these tales, is the significance of living. I understand this is a profound inquiry that has preoccupied scientists and philosophers for centuries. But after all my explorations, I've gotten closer than ever to finding the solution. The solution is revealed in the book's final section.

Do you ever wish you could break away from your regular life? So that you can broaden your horizons, expand your perspective, broaden your understanding of the world? I felt the same way when I first set out on my adventure as a travel photographer. However, I quickly realised that the conventional means of transportation weren't meeting my needs. I felt like I couldn't fully appreciate my travel destinations due to the constraints imposed by tour groups and hotels, the distance I needed to travel in rental cars and the lack of facilities to make my meals cost-effectively. I knew I had to step things up a notch at that point. It was a case of borrowing a line from Homegrown by Zac Brown Band and having everything I need and nothing that I don't.

I used my weekends to build the life I wanted, not escape the life I had. I didn't change who I was to match my surroundings. I simply picked better surroundings to be myself. Our brains are curious things, and they amplify what they're fed. It's vital that we feed our brains well and not focus our energy and time on negative things. If we do, we'll merely exacerbate that negativity. We need to stimulate our brains and souls to escape negativity, which is precisely what I did. Ultimately, you must remember that time is a gift. It's not something you're entitled to. And no matter how hard you try, you cannot control it/ The only thing you can do is choose how to spend the time you're given. Make good choices. You're so much more capable than you think. I promise. It might be challenging, but it's not impossible. You know all those things you want to do? You should do them.

I'll share some of my life's most formative and life-altering travel experiences within these pages. Each chapter provides a glimpse into a different time and place, from the crowded streets of New York City to the peaceful lakes of the Dolomites, from the rugged coastlines of Croatia to the majestic mountains of the Canadian Rockies.

Join me as I seek out the untrodden path and the answers to life's most profound questions. I make no pretence of being an all-knowing sage or guru. I am merely a wanderer seeking to understand myself and my place in the universe. However, I sincerely wish that my tales will serve as a source of encouragement, comfort, and pleasure for you. I hope you gain a fresh perspective and be inspired by the awe and wonder always present in our lives. You will be encouraged to embark on your own personal quest for knowledge. You will arrive at your own conclusions about the meaning of life. Oh, and before we get started, I'll address the biggest question about spending so much time alone on the road: - Don't you get lonely?

Being alone doesn't make you lonely

I'd much rather be alone than with the wrong company. I can feel lonelier with the wrong person than I'll ever feel by myself. OK, let's go.

THE MEANING OF LIFE

CHAPTER 1
FERNWEH

The Desire To Travel

There is a German word for the desire to go to other lands and see what lies beyond one's backyard. It's called "fernweh." It describes a feeling experienced by travellers over time and space and literally translates to 'far-sickness'. It's an unquenchable thirst for adventure. In contrast to homesickness, fernweh is a yearning for adventure and new experiences. It's a deep-down discontent, a craving for a variety of experiences and viewpoints that can be sated only by travelling.

The desire to see the world is vital in a lot of us. We fantasise about leaving on an epic journey, where we may learn about new cultures and make meaningful connections with interesting people (or even with ourselves) while searching for the answers to life's big questions. But what compels us to actively seek out such encounters? What compels us to forego the familiarity of our homes and set off on an adventure into the unknown?

It would appear that the answer can be found inside the fabric of the human soul. We as a species are insatiably inquisitive, ever on the prowl to expand our horizons and discover new things. The human race has always had an innate need to learn about its surroundings and make new discoveries. One of our most extraordinary skills is to observe and report. This is the very foundation of the news

— we observe the world around us and report back with our findings. We have always been curious about the world beyond our borders, whether it was the ancient Egyptians venturing up the Nile in quest of fresh riches or the Polynesians crossing the Pacific Ocean with only the stars for navigation.

Those of us who suffer from fernweh often have an overpowering yearning to see the world. We have an innate desire to explore the globe and broaden our horizons. We want to get away from the mundane routine of life and find out what it's all about. Despite our desire to see the world, we all have some innate need for familiar surroundings. Even when we set out on an adventure to discover the unknown, we long for what is known and loved back home. This contradiction is fundamental to being human, and the tug of war between the call of the road and the comforts of the home gives wanderlust its strength. What if I could find a solution?

Kofifernweh, my customised Mercedes Sprinter van, is where I've been living out my wanderlust dreams. My roaming home seemed fittingly named. Kofi is the Icelandic word for a cabin. Putting the two words together in this hybrid form means that Kofifernweh translates as 'the cabin with the desire to travel.'

I was able to give in to my wanderlust throughout my time in Kofifernweh. Without worrying about booking lodgings or joining a tour group, I could go wherever and whenever I pleased in my van. I could sleep under the stars in one location and wake up to the water in another. This allowed me to save money, eat well, experience the local culture, appreciate nature, and make friends with locals wherever I went. But Kofifernweh represented more than that; it embodied my yearning to see the world and all its wondrous diversity. It was a constant reminder that no matter how far I went or how many new places I visited, there was always more to learn and see.

Kofifernweh was my home on the road, my constant companion and shelter from the elements. It was a simple but functional space that allowed me the freedom to travel wherever my heart desired. And as I set out on the road with Kofifernweh, a van I converted in a friend's empty pub car park while the world was locked down, I felt a sense of liberation I had never experienced before.

Living in a van was a new experience for me, and it required a certain amount of adjustment. Vanlife, with its romantic allure of freedom and adventure, also presents its fair share of challenges. Living in a confined space on wheels requires a constant juggling act of practicality and minimalism. The most significant concern was water – I had 32 litres, and that was it. I need to stay in control and constantly be on the lookout for water sources to prevent the tank from going dry. Every aspect of daily life demands careful consideration and adaptation, from finding suitable places to park and sleep to managing limited resources such as water and electricity. The lack of stability and routine can be liberating and overwhelming as vanlifers navigate uncertain weather conditions, limited amenities, and the constant need to balance exploration with basic necessities. Yet, within these challenges, the true spirit of vanlife emerges, teaching resilience, resourcefulness, and an appreciation for the simplest of joys found along the open road. And many other challenges like continually being aware of wind speed and direction. Yes, this really matters.

As I settled into my cosy camper van amidst the vast open plains of southeast Iceland one December night, I braced myself for a night of turbulent winds. The gusts were known to be capable of picking up and hurling rocks and gravel with formidable force, presenting a unique challenge for a weary traveller seeking refuge. Aware of the risk of seasickness as the van was far less streamlined against the wind, I consciously decided to park with the back of the van facing the wind, prioritising the safety of my windscreen. In the early hours of the morning, as I lay in a state of restless sleep, I was abruptly jolted awake by the sheer force of the wind. I felt the van thrust forward, propelled by the invisible strength of nature's fury. The sound of gravel peppering the back and sides of the van was the soundtrack as, faster than I think I've ever moved. In a dazed state of being half-awake, I found myself in the driving seat some seven metres from where I'd been lying in bed. I hit the brakes and grabbed the steering wheel as my brain tried to process what was happening. The wind was fierce. It howled mercilessly, rattling the van and exerting a relentless pressure that overwhelmed even the firm grip of the handbrake. This was one example of a huge adjustment I had to make when I decided to live in a van to quench my thirst for adventure. You know when you're in a hotel room and aren't fully relaxed owing to your unfamiliar surroundings? That's human nature, and it's something that I carried with me. Almost everywhere I slept brought that feeling. Our sleep tends to be fragmented in unfamiliar surroundings, akin to how dolphins or horses rest. This is because our instinctual need for safety prompts our minds to remain partially awake, vigilant to potential security threats in unfamiliar environments. Even as we drift into slumber, a part of our consciousness remains alert, attuned to the unfamiliar sounds and sensations surrounding us, ensuring our safety and allowing us to respond swiftly if needed. It is an adaptive response ingrained within us. This subconscious defence mechanism acknowledges the importance of staying aware in new and potentially unpredictable settings. Living in the van and constantly moving meant almost every night was like that. Because of my semi-conscious state, I could react so quickly without even thinking about it. That night in Iceland was a humbling reminder of the raw power surrounding me and the unpredictable nature of the elements in this rugged and beautiful land.

Other vanlife considerations include constantly taking note of places that could serve as a good park-up. Noting level surfaces that gave me a night in a flat bed rather than one on a slope, waking up sore, and never-ending temperature management skills are things I didn't realise were so essential. Despite this, it also allowed me a level of flexibility and freedom that I had never experienced before. I could travel at my own pace, take detours whenever I wanted, and truly immerse myself in the places I visited.

As I travelled in Kofifernweh, I discovered that the world was full of hidden treasures, secret corners, and unexpected surprises. Every day was a new adventure and opportunity to explore, learn, and grow. And as I travelled, I came to understand the true nature of wanderlust. It was not just a desire to travel for the sake of it but a deep and abiding love for the world and all its wonders. It was a desire to see, experience, and connect with the world in a profound and transformative way.

Through my travels, I have come to understand that wanderlust is not just a desire to see new places but a way of life. It is a way of embracing the world with open arms, seeking new experiences, and living life to the fullest. I soon realised that life begins at the end of your comfort zone. We often hear the age-old saying, 'Good things come to those who wait,' but this simply isn't true. Good things come to those who go out and fucking earn it. I'd travelled extensively already, but Kofifernweh took things to a different level.

I have also come to understand that wanderlust is not just a solitary pursuit but a shared experience. The people I have met on my travels have enriched my life in countless ways and taught me the value of human connection and community. Through travel, I truly learned to see and realise that everything connects to everything else.

From this vanlife experience, as I continue to travel and explore the world, I do so with a sense of joy and wonder and with a deep appreciation for the beauty and complexity of the world we live in. We all get dealt different cards, but it's important to remember that we don't play the cards – we play the game. We get what everyone else gets. We get a lifetime. It's up to us what we do with it.

Travel is not just a passion but a way of life. It is a way of seeing the world, understanding ourselves, and embracing the infinite possibilities that life has to offer. And as I continue on my journey, I know that I am exactly where I am meant to be, living my life to the fullest and enjoying every moment of the adventure. Even when the road got rough, believing anything was possible kept me going. It was tiresome because there were so many roadblocks. My urge to see the world wasn't something I felt occasionally; rather, it was ingrained in my very being.

But why is it that travelling overseas is so appealing? Why do we feel the need to travel the world and learn about different cultures? Many people see travel as an opportunity to get away from their regular lives. It's a chance to spend time in a stimulating setting without worrying about responsibilities at home, school, or work. But going on a trip is about more than just getting away from your routine. It's a great way to broaden one's perspectives and learn more about the globe.

When we travel, we get to know different societies and their customs. In doing so, we broaden our understanding of the world and its many ways of life, as well as the depth and variety of the human experience. Our personal prejudices and assumptions can be tested to the fullest extent when we travel. There is no substitute for first-hand experience when it comes to learning about a new culture or location. To this end, travel has the potential to be a profound catalyst for change and development. It can help us develop greater tolerance, compassion, and self-awareness. The journey itself is often more important than the destination. Along the journey, there are many powerful moments. These moments should themselves be cherished because sometimes, you will never know the true value of a moment until it becomes a memory.

There are always difficulties to face when travelling. There will be times when you miss home or feel lonely, when learning a new language is difficult, or when you face unexpected challenges. However, these tests are what make travel so worthwhile. In the face of adversity, we learn and grow the most; in these times of testing, we find our inner fortitude and resilience.

Kofifernweh was the ideal means to satisfy my desire to see the world. It allowed me to travel the world at my own pace, deciding where I wanted to go and how I wanted to get there. It represented my aspiration to seize every opportunity and see as much of the world as possible. More importantly, though, it served as a reminder that the route might be as rewarding as the final destination. The things we learn along the journey are more important than the destinations we visit or the activities we partake in.

So, I am filled with awe and appreciation for all I have seen and experienced as I continue to travel and discover the world around me. I appreciate all the experiences I've had and the friends I've made along the road.

My insatiable curiosity about the globe and the opportunities it holds has given me a permanent case of the travel bug. As a result, I'm constantly on the lookout for novel experiences and expanding my horizons to accommodate this hunger. It was a risk. A huge risk. But I was constantly reminded that I shouldn't be afraid to fail. I should be afraid not to try. Retrospectively I now know something even more potent in relation to failure versus strength: - Be strong. You never know who you are inspiring.

This is your life. Do what you love and do it often. If you don't like something, change it. If you're in the wrong job, quit. If you feel like you don't have enough time, stop watching TV and get outside. If you're looking for the love of your life, stop; they will be waiting for you when you start doing the things you love and being yourself. Stop over-complicating things – life is simple. Open your mind, your arms, and your heart to new things. Appreciate that we are all different, but those very differences can be the things that unite us. Share your passion and ask the person beside you what their passion is. Create something. Anything. Getting lost will help you find yourself, so travel often. Some opportunities come once in a lifetime, so seize them.

Oh, and when I say travel, I don't mean staying at fancy resorts and buying trinkets from souvenir stores to serve as evidence you were there. I mean, really explore another place. Become a part of it. Sit in coffee shops tucked away on hidden streets and observe the world passing by, looking for lessons to learn. Hike mountains, stroll along beaches, and meet people unlike you. Sometimes you'll find yourself in the middle of nowhere, but sometimes, in the middle of nowhere, you'll find yourself. See the world through fresh eyes with the ability to return home with a map and point out these places, each having a story of how these places changed you. It isn't about Instagram-famous locations. It's about hidden secrets and real life. Create the ability to reflect on life, saying, "I can't believe I did that" instead of "If only

I had." Life is short. Live your dream, share your passion, and once in a lifetime, as often as you can.

I didn't start in the van – the van was the solution to my problem. I was initially chasing my dream of shooting photos worthy of National Geographic while working a regular day job. I was travelling on my days off and constantly working on improving as a photographer. I was travelling internationally approximately 18 times every year, and I had to make a choice for my own mental and physical health. One of these things had to go: the day job or the travel. The answer was obvious, but I needed a little extra courage to make the jump.

As I continued to travel and explore the world, I reaffirmed that my desire to see new places and experience new things was not just a passing phase but a fundamental part of who I was. I yearned to see the world, explore its vast and varied landscapes, and immerse myself in its diverse cultures and traditions. For me, travel was a way of breaking free from the routine and monotony of everyday life. It was a chance to push my boundaries, challenge myself, and discover my strengths and limitations. Despite my love of travel, I still felt trapped in a day job that left me unfulfilled and uninspired. I knew I needed to make a change, take a risk and follow my passion for photography and writing, but I was afraid of what that might entail.

Eventually, the call of the open road became too strong to ignore. I left my day job and embarked on a journey of self-discovery, travelling the world and capturing its beauty through the lens of my camera. Here's the craziest revelation

I made, however. I learned that my camera is a tool for learning to see without a camera. My camera was almost an excuse, giving me a reason to visit some beautiful places, but only without my camera was I really able to see.

It was a bold and empowering decision that allowed me to focus on the things that truly mattered to me. I was able to immerse myself fully in my photography and writing, hone my skills and develop my craft, and create something that was indeed my own. But more than that, it was a chance to experience the world in a way I had never thought possible. I was able to travel at my own pace, to chart my own course, and to see the world on my own terms.

And as I travelled, I realised that the rewards of travel went far beyond the simple pleasures of seeing new places and meeting new people. It was a chance to broaden my horizons, challenge my assumptions, and gain a deeper understanding of the world around me.

Through my travels, I learned about the diversity of human experience, the beauty of different cultures and traditions, and the common threads that connect us all as human beings. I discovered that travel was not just a way of escaping the routine of everyday life but a way of embracing it fully, of living each moment to the fullest and savouring every experience as it came.

Ultimately, I discovered that the only way to truly live was to follow my passions, pursue my dreams, and embrace the world with open arms. And while the road ahead may be uncertain and full of challenges, I know that I am on the right path, living my life to the fullest, and I wouldn't have it any other way. The biggest adventure you can undertake is to live the life of your dreams. If I could offer one piece of advice after what I've done it's this: Embrace the grandest adventure of living your dreams, guided not by fears, but by the unwavering passion within your heart. Your dreams know the way.

CHAPTER 2
UBUNTU

The Spirit Of Humanity

The sun was setting over the Indian Ocean, and the sky was ablaze. I was sitting on a rocky outcrop, watching in awe as a pod of Southern Right Whales frolicked in the waves below the rocks, spy-hopping and fluking. It was a magical moment, one that would stay with me forever.

Before vanlife and even before I was a police officer, I lived in Franskraal, a small town on the coast of the Western Cape in South Africa. It was here that my love for travel and adventure had truly taken root and where I first discovered the true spirit of humanity, embodied in the word ubuntu.

Ubuntu is a Xhosa word that roughly translates to "I am because we are." It is a concept deeply rooted in African culture and celebrates the interconnectedness of all living things. It is the word for 'human-ness.' It is a philosophy that recognises that we are all part of a greater whole and that our actions have a ripple effect that extends far beyond our individual lives.

As I travelled through South Africa, I encountered countless examples of ubuntu in action. From the Xhosa people I met in the Western Cape, who welcomed me into their homes with open arms, to the meerkat whisperer in the

Karoo, who showed me the true meaning of dedication and connection.

One of my most unforgettable experiences was on one of many safaris. As I sat in a jeep, watching a herd of elephants cavorting in a waterhole, I felt a deep sense of connection to the natural world around me. It was a moment of pure magic, one that reminded me of the beauty and complexity of the world we live in. The overwhelming thought that raced through my mind was that of communication. These elephants had only expressions and actions to share their thoughts and feelings, but we have the power of words. Words carry more power than we realise, and we should use them wisely. I'll confidently say that if you see something beautiful in someone else, tell them. Your words may last them a lifetime.

Ubuntu is not just about our connection to each other. It is also about our connection to the natural world. One of my most challenging and rewarding experiences in South Africa was when I went shark cage diving. The trepidation turned out to be nothing to worry about, and in fact, I went back several times to swim with the sharks. As I plunged into the icy waters of the Atlantic, I was terrified and exhilarated in equal measure. But as I gazed into the eyes of a Great White shark, I felt a sense of awe and wonder that transcended fear.

As we made our way out to sea, I could feel my heart racing with anticipation. We anchored the boat and prepared to enter the water. I couldn't help but feel a sense of trepidation. The water was murky and dark, and the thought of coming face-to-face with a great white shark was both thrilling and terrifying. I had always been fascinated by sharks, and the opportunity to get up close and personal with these majestic creatures was something I simply couldn't pass up.

But as I slipped into the shark cage and lowered myself into the water, I felt a rush of adrenaline like nothing else. The sharks were initially slow to approach, but as the crew began to chum the water with fish, they soon started to circle around us. My eyes were transfixed upon their sharp teeth gleaming in the sunlight. The chum was made of the local fishing industry's discarded by-product, creating a mess in the water. The nearby Dyer Island and Geyser Rock created what was known internationally as the drive-thru of the shark world. Sharks could swim through the narrow strait in this place for a guaranteed seal meal.

Despite the fear and excitement I felt, I also couldn't help but be struck by the beauty of these creatures. They moved with an effortless grace, their powerful bodies gliding through the water quickly. As I watched these magnificent animals swim past me, I felt a sense of awe and wonder at the sheer power and majesty of the natural world. It was an experience I will never forget.

It was at this moment that I realised the true power of ubuntu. Even in the face of danger and uncertainty, a sense of shared humanity always binds us. It is a sense of connection that extends far beyond our individual lives and reminds us of the power of community and compassion. I knew that the Great White Shark I swam with, measuring at least 20ft in length, was literally able to see my fear. The ampullae of Lorenzini that pitted its snout detected tiny electric currents, including my heart beating. Harmonising with nature and knowing there was support from the other people in the boat gave me the strength to appreciate the moment for its value. I was connected to nature. Sure, the nature I was connected with had such archaic power that it was immune to cancer and could smell a drop of blood in the sea. It just happened to have bone-crushing jaws lined with serrated razors, but it was nature, and I was connected with it. It knew I wasn't food.

One of the most fascinating experiences I had while travelling through South Africa was waking up early to watch a family of meerkats emerge from their burrows in the Klein Karoo. I had heard about a man named Grant McIlrath, who had been dubbed "The Meerkat Man" for his expertise in working with these fascinating animals, and I knew I had to see them for myself.

As I arrived at the meerkat den site just before sunrise, I could feel the excitement building in my chest. I knew these animals were notoriously skittish and that getting too close could scare them off. But as Grant led us to a spot where we could watch the meerkats from a safe distance, I felt a sense of awe and wonder wash over me. Grant had built a relationship with these meerkats. They trusted him, and I was about to witness their connection.

At first, the meerkats were barely visible in the dim light of dawn as they poked their heads out of their burrows and scanned the horizon for predators. But as the sun began to rise, they increasingly emerged, stretching their legs and grooming each other with delicate fingers.

Watching these creatures go about their morning routine was like witnessing a miniature society in action. I could see the hierarchy at play as the dominant male kept a watchful eye on the rest of the group. At the same time, the females scurried around, collecting food and caring for their young.

As the sun climbed higher in the sky, the meerkats grew bolder and more active, darting back and forth across the sandy terrain with remarkable speed and agility. I felt grateful to have witnessed this rare glimpse into their world.

Reflecting on my eight months in South Africa, I am struck by the profound sense of ubuntu that pervades every aspect of life. A spirit of generosity, compassion, and connection is at the heart of African culture. It has the power to transform lives and communities.

For me, ubuntu is not just a word but a lifestyle. It is a reminder of the interconnectedness of all living things and of the importance of compassion and connection in a world that often feels disconnected and divided.

Now, as I continue to travel and explore the world, I carry the spirit of ubuntu with me always. It is a reminder that no matter where we go or what we do, we are all part of a greater whole and that our actions have the power to shape the world in ways we may never fully understand. We speak different languages, we look different, we eat differently, but ultimately, we're all the same.

So, as I sit here, replaying the sunset over the Indian Ocean in my mind again, I am filled with a sense of gratitude and wonder for the beauty and complexity of our world. I am reminded, once again, of the power of ubuntu and the spirit of humanity that connects us all. Ubuntu is about recognising the inherent dignity and worth of every human being and understanding that we are all connected in a fundamental way.

In the Xhosa culture, ubuntu is expressed through the concept of "umuntu ngumuntu ngabantu," which means "a person is a person through other people." This idea emphasises the importance of community and interdependence and the belief that we cannot truly be fulfilled or successful on our own. Instead, we are all part of a larger whole, and our actions and choices have a ripple effect that extends far beyond ourselves. We are all part of something greater than ourselves and that by treating each other with kindness and respect, we can create a more just, compassionate, and fulfilling world.

CHAPTER 3
ÞETTA REDDAST

Everything Will Work Out Alright

The Icelandic phrase 'Thetta Reddast' was one that I first heard when I found myself in a bit of a predicament while on a photography trip in Iceland. I had travelled to the country to photograph arctic foxes named Ingi and Mori at the Arctic Fox Centre, but on the day before the shoot, disaster struck.

Gljúfrabúi is a hidden gem nestled within the picturesque landscapes of Iceland. Many people miss it because of its proximity to Seljalandsfoss, a famous waterfall. Known as the "hidden waterfall" or "canyon waterfall," Gljúfrabúi resides within a narrow gorge, partially concealed by towering cliffs and verdant vegetation. It is a mesmerising waterfall that holds a touch of mystery and enchantment. The ambience within the hidden realm of Gljúfrabúi is enchanting as if stepping into a secret sanctuary untouched by time. Moss-covered walls, lush ferns, and glistening rocks surround the intimate space, adding to the otherworldly atmosphere. The air rushes past, and the space is filled with the melody of fast, falling water, creating a soothing symphony that resonates with the soul. To truly experience this natural wonder, one must venture into the narrow opening of the cliff, carefully navigating through a shallow stream and stepping onto slippery rocks. Inside the cavern, a magnificent sight unfolds—a slender cascade gracefully descends from a lofty height, enveloped in a veil of mist and illuminated by the soft glow of natural light. I had to get a photo in this spot with myself standing on a rock in the foreground to show scale, so I decided to venture closer to Gljúfrabúi. I was rewarded with a captivating display of nature's raw power and beauty. The water cascades with force, creating a mesmerising dance of fluidity and grace. The water's sheer intensity and pristine clarity captivate the senses, leaving an indelible impression on all who witness its grandeur and, in my case, penetrates deep into the camera, as you'll find out. It all seemed fine, and at first glance, it looked as if all I needed to do was dry the camera out. It appeared merely cosmetic. I thought it was wet.

I hit the road to drive 335 miles (543km) up to Súðavik, in the Westfjords, where I was first due to meet Ingi and Mori. I was also due to take a helicopter flight with Norðurflug the following day. I had to dry my gear and be ready. I had the camera on the dash for the entire drive with all the ports open and the battery and memory card ejected. If I could get warm air into the camera, it would dry out and be fine, right? Wrong.

The monumental drive was going well. The accommodation that night was in Ïsafjörður. Shortly after arriving, a quick camera test revealed more to my problem than just a wet camera. With the battery back in place and the camera powered on, I noted a few glitches here and there, but ultimately, everything still worked. It was good enough. I now firmly believe that good enough isn't good enough, and perhaps this is the origin of that philosophy.

That evening the northern lights exploded and filled the night sky. I found myself in the prime position on a mountain pass atop one of the Westfjords' stunning, jagged snow peaks. In the sky above me, lady aurora flowed at full strength. It caused the snow to glow green and juxtaposed the static Milky Way that lingered and spanned from one horizon to another. I became immune to the cold, as is always the case when the night sky fills with a stunning light show. I had my camera on the tripod and took only a few photos. To my surprise, the camera began shooting by itself. I heard the mirror slap and the curtain slide as frames were created without my input. Little did I know, these would be the last photos this camera would ever take.

That evening in the hotel, I kept the camera on the radiator all night, and rice was the weapon of choice the following morning. I immediately put the camera back on the dash with the heaters on, wrapped loosely in a travel towel in an attempt to soak in any moisture I'd missed. None of it worked. I later discovered that this camera sat in a category entitled 'beyond economical repair', and my cheapest option was buying a new one. Let's not get ahead of ourselves, though.

When I arrived at the Arctic Fox Centre, I had to sheepishly explain my predicament to Midge, the zoologist who ran the place. Then, as the coffee pot went on, I was introduced to the concept of 'Thetta Reddast.' The phrase, which translates roughly to 'it will all work out,' is a common saying in Iceland. It encapsulates the country's laid-back and optimistic outlook on life. I guess it makes sense when you're surrounded by volcanos that could erupt at any moment on a barren landscape full of anomalies such as deep caverns, boiling mud, raging rivers, and a weather system so famously irrational that most Icelanders will tell you that if you don't like the weather, just wait five minutes.

Back to the problem at hand, I was in overdrive trying to come up with a solution and the words 'Thetta Reddast' meant nothing to me. As a registered Nikon Professional, I was able to pull some strings and use this privileged position to my advantage. The next problem was, after speaking to Nikon on the phone, that their only available solution was to send me a camera from Sweden. They were about to do it and the news was elating but short-lived since, being in the remote location I was making the call from, their camera would be with me in four days despite their willingness to drive it to the airport and put it on the next flight. The problem lay on my side of things – an international arrival into Keflavík would need to then be couriered to Reykjavík and put on an internal flight to Ísafjörður. They were willing to help me, but the help wouldn't arrive in time. Despite my worries, I was assured that everything would work out and that I could find a solution to my camera problem. Some more calls followed to local photographers and the local tourist board. Sure enough, someone was able to lend me a camera to use, saving the trip and allowing me to capture some incredible images of Ingi and Mori.

With my camera troubles behind me, I was able to explore Iceland's southwest peninsula from a helicopter with Norðurflug. The aerial views of the rugged coastline, icy glaciers, dormant volcano cones, and bubbling hot springs were simply astonishing. As I flew over the landscape, I couldn't help but think back to the concept of 'Thetta Reddast.' Here's the craziest part: the expansive lava field below was constructed of lava tubes that showed the path the magma took some 800-900 years ago when this landscape was formed from a volcanic eruption. Right in the middle of the lave channels was an enormous heart. It's as if that heart was Thor's way of reminding me that everything does work out fine. It was a reminder that no matter what challenges we may face in life, there is always a way forward and things have a way of working themselves out in the end.

The whole experience left me feeling inspired and grateful. It taught me the importance of embracing the unexpected and having faith that everything will work out in the end.

I'm constantly reminded of the concept of "Thetta Reddast.' Whether navigating icy roads in the middle of a snowstorm or dealing with unexpected travel delays, I learned to take a deep breath and trust that everything would work out in the end.

I've returned to Iceland over twenty times. The landscape is incredible, as are the people. One place almost every trip to Iceland takes in is the town of Vík, famous for its black sand beaches and towering sea stacks. This place is perfect for demonstrating the power of nature and the importance of respecting the environment. As you stand on the beach, watching the waves crash against the shore and feeling the wind whip through your hair, you'll be struck by the sheer force of nature. It serves as a reminder that we are just small, fleeting beings in the grand scheme of things and have a responsibility to protect and preserve the planet we call home.

Despite the challenges and moments of reflection, my trip to Iceland that killed my camera was filled with joy and wonder. From watching the Northern Lights dance across the night sky to soaking in the warm waters of a natural hot spring, I was constantly reminded of the beauty and magic of the world around us. It was all made possible by the 'Thetta Reddast' concept - a reminder to trust in the journey and have faith that everything will work out in the end.

As my time in Iceland came to a close, I felt a sense of deep gratitude for the experiences I had had and the lessons I had learned. And while my journey may have been filled with twists and turns, I knew that I had come out the other side a stronger and more resilient person.

For anyone who has ever felt the call of wanderlust or the desire to explore the world, I can only offer one piece of advice: embrace the journey and trust in the power of 'Thetta Reddast.'

CHAPTER 4
SISU

Courage And Determination In The Face Of Adversity

As a traveller, I have always been drawn to places that challenge me - both physically and mentally. And nowhere was this more true than during my time in Finland, where I was introduced to the Finnish concept of 'sisu.'

At its core, 'sisu' is about resilience and perseverance in the face of adversity. It's about digging deep and finding the strength to push through even when things seem impossible. There were few times in my travels when I needed 'sisu' more than when I spent a night in my van, Kofifernweh, in the Pallas-Yllästunturi National Park in the dead of winter.

The temperature that night was a bone-chilling -38°C. Even with all the insulation and heating elements in the van, it was a constant battle to stay warm. The diesel fuel began to crystalise and become thick and sludgy, and the batteries struggled to hold a charge in the frigid temperatures. Despite the challenges, I was determined to stick it out. I knew this was an opportunity to push myself and test my limits, to see how far my 'sisu' could take me.

My first clue that the temperature would be crazy-low involved my hand sticking to my tripod when I retrieved my rig. It was outside shooting a timelapse of a band of aurora causally spanning the entire sky, pulsing gently under the moonlight. That crystal clear sky and the still, dry air were the perfect formulae for extreme cold. I watched my thermometer slowly drop past -25°C. At each point on the scale, I grabbed a picture thinking, surely it can't get colder; this has to be a record for me. As the night wore on, I constantly checked the van's gauges and monitored its systems. Keeping the mechanical elements functioning in the extreme cold was a never-ending battle. Soon enough, the thermometer hit -38°C, and everything changed. The thermometer stopped working, so the temperature may even have dropped further. This was no longer an adventure I was documenting for my little YouTube channel – it was an actual survival scene. Temperatures this low can easily be a killer. All manner of thoughts raced through my mind. On the left of my brain, I was going through all my logical thoughts: where is the nearest town? It's Muonio, 29km away. What temperature does the diesel freeze at? How thick is the fuel pipe to my heater? Is it insulated enough? What about the brakes? Will they freeze on? Meanwhile, in my right brain, the emotional response fired up. Time. Remember, it's a gift. Not something you're entitled to. No matter how hard you try, you can't control it. The only thing you can do is choose how to spend the time you're given. That was it – I cranked up the heater to ensure the van stayed warm. I put on all the layers I could, and out I went. Wading through waist-deep powder snow was the next thing I knew. At that extreme temperature, everything felt pretty much the same, and I knew the insulating power of snow, so I found a good spot and laid back. As I lay on my back in the powder, surrounded by the resonating stillness of a frozen Lapland, the biting cold kissed my cheeks, reminding me of the immensity of the Arctic winter. Above me, the night sky erupted with a dance of vibrant colours as the Northern Lights painted their cosmic strokes across the heavens. Time seemed to stand still as I gazed upward, mesmerised by the celestial spectacle. The frozen forest encircling me stood as a silent witness. The snow-covered branches of the pine reaching toward the stars. At that moment, amidst the bone-chilling cold, I felt a profound connection to the wild beauty of the Arctic, a humbling reminder of the awe-inspiring wonders that nature holds. I was reminded of two words I constantly heard in my past life as a yoga photographer. Present, and why.

'Why' is a great word we should use for every decision we make? It's so important to find your 'why?' Why are you doing this? From a philosophical perspective, the question of "why" is essential to understanding the purpose and meaning behind our actions. The power of why lies in its ability to challenge assumptions and unearth deeper motivations that may not be immediately apparent. By questioning why we do anything, we can gain insight into our values, beliefs, and desires and make more intentional choices that align with our personal goals and ideals. Without considering why, we risk operating on autopilot, allowing external factors or societal norms to dictate our behaviour without critical examination. Embracing the power of why requires courage and self-reflection, but it ultimately leads to a more fulfilling and authentic life. And so the other word: 'present.'

The word "present" carries a powerful meaning, reminding us of the importance of fully engaging in the moment. To be present is to cultivate a sense of mindfulness, to bring our attention to the here and now, and to let go of past regrets or future anxieties. It is a mindset that can help us fully appreciate life's beauty and wonder, connect more deeply with others, and find greater meaning and purpose in our daily activities. When we are present, we can engage in life with a sense of curiosity and openness. We are more likely to seize opportunities that will help us grow and improve.

Taking every opportunity that will improve us is an essential part of being present. It means being proactive, seeking out new experiences and challenges, and embracing opportunities for personal and professional development. By being present in the moment and actively seeking out opportunities to improve ourselves, we can expand our horizons, develop new skills and talents, and grow into the best versions of ourselves. Whether taking a new course, learning a new language, or stepping out of our comfort zones to try something new, the willingness to take advantage of every opportunity is a powerful way to live life to the fullest. By combining the power of presence with a growth mindset, we can unlock our full potential and create a life of meaning and purpose.

As I lay under several blankets, noticing the frost form on the few areas of exposed metal inside the van, hearing nothing but stillness from outside and feeling the warmth of my breath against my face, I was struck by the raw beauty of the winter landscape. The stars shone like diamonds in the sky, and the snow-covered trees glimmered in the moonlight. It was a reminder that even in the harshest of environments, beauty still exists. As difficult as the night was, it was also enriching. I was present, and I had my reason why. Sisu had made it possible.

As the first light of dawn crept over the horizon, I felt a sense of deep satisfaction and accomplishment. I had pushed myself to the limits of my endurance, and I had come out the other side more robust and more resilient.

Looking back on that night, I am grateful for the lessons that 'sisu' taught me. It's a reminder that no matter how challenging a situation may seem, there is always a way if you have the strength and determination to persevere. It's a lesson I carry with me as I continue exploring the world and seeking new adventures. Because no matter where my travels may take me, I know that I have the 'sisu' to face any challenge that comes my way.

Sisu followed me, and my resilience was tested heavily during portions of my 'Schengen Shuffle' after my first Due North adventure. In contrast to the polar experience I'd enjoyed for the preceding few months, I embarked on a journey filled with rich scenery, rich history, and unexpected encounters. The road took me through the diverse landscapes of Germany, Austria, Slovenia, Croatia, and the Balkans to Bulgaria and Romania. However, amidst the beauty and charm of these countries, a sobering reality revealed itself on the highways and roads. A sight that left an indelible mark on my journey was the presence of military convoys, transporting tanks and armoured vehicles on the backs of trucks, a visible sign of Europe's preparedness in response to the impending invasion of Ukraine.

As I drove along the highways of Europe, the engine's hum accompanied my thoughts, and my gaze was drawn to the formidable presence of military convoys that began to appear traversing the same roads. Seeing the tanks and armoured vehicles nestled atop the trucks evoked a sense of sombre anticipation. The scene was a stark reminder that geopolitical tensions loomed heavily in the collective consciousness beyond the picturesque landscapes and the warmth of the local cultures.

The convoy blended seamlessly with the orderly traffic flow in Germany, known for its efficiency and precision. The sight of such machinery juxtaposed against the backdrop of autobahns symbolised a nation's commitment to protecting its interests and ensuring the safety of its allies. It served as a tangible reminder that peace and stability should not be taken for granted.

As I ventured into Romania, the sight of the convoy held a different significance. It echoed the nation's tumultuous history and the scars left by past conflicts. The presence of military preparedness carried a sense of determination, a resolute stand against any encroachment upon the sovereignty of neighbouring nations. It was a poignant reminder that even in a world striving for harmony, the echoes of past conflicts continue to reverberate.

The spectre of an impending invasion of Ukraine loomed large during this journey. While jarring, the sight of the military convoys served as a reminder of the importance of diplomacy, international cooperation, and the pursuit of peaceful resolutions. It was a chilling reminder that peace is fragile and geopolitical tensions can disrupt the tranquillity we often take for granted.

With this on my mind and while trying to make the most of an air that carried the weight of tension, I had an experience I knew I risked facing for a long time. I awoke with a start, jolted from my peaceful slumber by the piercing sound of metal against metal. It was 4 am in rural Serbia, and my world was cloaked in darkness. Confusion and fear flooded my senses as the reality of the situation slowly dawned upon me. Someone was breaking into the back door of my van. My heart raced, pounding in my chest like a war drum, as adrenaline surged through my veins. Kofifernweh has a huge, obvious solar panel and skylight. Each side of the van is adorned with vinyl decals of my name and the Kofifernweh logo. This is quite clearly a camper conversion, and it was surely obvious that there would be someone inside, right?

With cautious haste, I pushed myself up from the bed, my senses heightened and my mind racing to comprehend the imminent danger. The cold air seeped through the cracks, sending shivers down my spine as I fumbled for a light source. The feeble glow of my flashlight illuminated the interior of the van, casting eerie shadows across the cramped space. As I tiptoed towards the side door, the distinct sound of the rear door lock being forced echoed through the silence. Panic and anger intertwined within me, giving birth to newfound courage. With each step, my heartbeats synchronised with the menacing rhythm of my breath. Determination flooded my being as I prepared to confront the intruders.

With a resounding crash, I slammed the side door open, revealing two silhouettes against the darkness at the back of the van. The flickering beam of my flashlight illuminated their faces, their features twisted by a combination of surprise and malevolence. In their hands, hammers and screwdrivers were my threat. Time seemed to slow as our eyes locked, and an unspoken battle of wills ensued. At that moment, the fear melted away, replaced by a primal instinct to protect what was rightfully mine. With a guttural roar, I lunged forward, my body propelled by a surge of adrenaline. The intruders recoiled, their initial bravado fading into desperation as they stumbled backwards, their intentions laid bare. It was warm so I was in nothing but my boxer shorts, which probably went a long way to winning the fight already.

Through my rage, a fierce determination fuelled my pursuit. We darted through the rest area, shadows dancing in the moonlit night, my heart pounding with the urgency of the chase. The dance of their feet kicking up gravel as they moved to escape echoed against the stillness of the rural Serbian landscape, a chilling soundtrack to the adrenaline-fueled pursuit.

Breathless and fuelled by terror and courage, I watched them disappear into the darkness along the road, their figures blending seamlessly with the night. Exhaustion seeped into my bones, mingling with the residue of fear and exhilaration that coursed through my veins. I stood alone in the darkness, the echoes of the encounter lingering in the air. Realising I'd left my keys inside the van I made my way back, knowing I wouldn't stay for the rest of the night. With trembling hands and racing thoughts, I gathered my belongings, acutely aware that the sanctity of my temporary sanctuary had been shattered. Once a place of solace and respite, the rest area I was parked in now carried an ominous weight. Every creak and whisper of the night became a reminder of the vulnerability and the unpredictability of the world.

As I drove away from that rest area, the adrenaline slowly subsided, and a newfound sense of vigilance settled within me. The encounter had left an indelible mark, a reminder that darkness can lurk even in the most unexpected places. But amidst the fear and uncertainty, a spark of resilience flickered within me, reminding me of the strength in confronting adversity head-on. I carried a lot of experience from my past as a police officer but this time instead of protecting the property of others, it was my own.

From that night forward, I carried with me not just the memory of the harrowing encounter but also a renewed sense of awareness and an unwavering determination to protect myself. The incident had transformed me, leaving me with a newfound appreciation for the fragility of safety and a heightened sense of vigilance in a world that can sometimes be cruel and unforgiving.

As I continued my travels through these countries, the memories of the military convoys lingered, along with that of the break-in. They cast a shadow over the beauty of the landscapes, challenging the notion of an idyllic world. Yet, amidst the uncertainty, there was hope—the hope that the drums of war could be silenced through dialogue, understanding, and a shared commitment to peace. The world could strive towards a future where such convoys become relics of the past. I was now in Romania traversing the Carpathian Mountain Range and visiting Dracula's Castle.

As the shadows of uncertainty loomed more significantly with each passing mile, I faced a difficult decision. I had to cut my journey short and drive back from Romania to the UK. The proximity to Ukraine and the intensifying presence of military convoys weighed heavily on my mind. In the face of potential conflict, I knew that prioritising safety and well-being was paramount, even if it meant undertaking an incredible challenge.

The drive became a test of endurance, both physical and emotional. Time slipped away, the hours blurring together as I pressed on, driven by a singular purpose. The challenge of completing the journey within 24 hours weighed heavily on my shoulders, yet a resolute determination propelled me forward. I only had 24 hours because out of the 90-day allowance for travel in the Schengen Area in a post-Brexit world, I was on day 89. My decision was compounded when the scale of the military convoys apparently grew.

With a heavy heart and a sense of trepidation, I embarked on the arduous journey back, knowing that time was of the essence. The road stretched out before me, a seemingly endless ribbon connecting the countries I had traversed. The situation's urgency propelled me forward, pushing past fatigue and testing my resolve.

As I drove around the outskirts of Budapest, the intensity of the military convoys increased, amplifying the gravity of the situation. The roads buzzed with the synchronised movement of armoured vehicles, a visible reminder of the tensions gripping the region. It was a chilling affirmation that the decision to turn back was indeed correct. The realisation washed over me, mingling with relief that I had chosen prudence over adventure. I had to make a difficult decision to cut my trip short and use the one day I still had in the bank to get back across the Schengen Area to the relative safety of the UK.

As the miles ticked away, the landscape transformed, and the echoes of unfamiliar languages gradually faded. I found solace in the familiar signs and landmarks that signalled my approach to the UK. The journey became metaphorical, mirroring the resilience and strength required to navigate uncertain times.

Finally, as I reached the shores of the UK, a sense of accomplishment washed over me. The drive had been gruelling, but prioritising safety and return had proven its worth. The challenges I faced along the way paled in comparison to the reassurance that I had taken the necessary steps to protect myself. I was also able to pay a visit to Pete, the world's best mechanic, to get my back door fixed.

Looking back, I carried with me the memories of the incredible landscapes and cultural encounters and a deeper appreciation for the delicate balance between adventure and caution. I had been reminded of the unpredictability of the world and the importance of heeding the signs and making decisions in the best interest of well-being. Though my journey had been cut short, the experience was a powerful reminder of the value of flexibility, adaptability, and the innate human drive to overcome obstacles. It affirmed the notion that sometimes the most extraordinary challenges are the ones that shape us the most profoundly, leaving us with a renewed sense of resilience and a deeper understanding of the interconnectedness of our global community.

In our journey through life, we will undoubtedly face numerous setbacks and defeats. We must refuse to let these moments define us. In fact, these defeats may serve as valuable stepping stones towards self-discovery and personal growth. They reveal our true character and teach us what we are capable of overcoming. Remember, the struggles we endure today will one day become cherished memories we laugh about, reminiscing on the strength and resilience that carried us through. Through the most brutal battles, our triumphs shine the brightest, reminding us that the greater the struggle, the more glorious the victory.

CHAPTER 5
HIRAETH

Homesickness For A Home To Which You Cannot Return

This Welsh word captures the essence of a feeling I've carried with me for as long as I can remember. It's a longing, a nostalgia for a place that perhaps doesn't exist. A yearning for a home that never was, and yet somehow, it's always been there, lurking in the recesses of my heart. Hiraeth is the anchor of my existence, a constant reminder that I don't belong to just one place but to many.

As a travel photographer, I've had the privilege of exploring the world and capturing its beauty through my lens. I've witnessed the most beautiful sunsets in the deserts of South Africa, danced under the vibrant lights of New York City, and wandered through the bustling markets of Marrakech. Each place I've visited has left an indelible mark on my soul, but each time I returned it didn't feel as if I was arriving home. They were temporary havens, fulfilling my desire for adventure and discovery but never quenching the thirst for a place to call my own.

During my journeys through Scandinavia, I felt the first stirrings of a deeper connection. The rugged landscapes of Iceland spoke to me in a language I could not comprehend yet understood with every fibre of my being. The roaring waterfalls cascading down moss-covered cliffs, the ethereal dance of the Northern Lights in the night sky—they whispered secrets that resonated deep within me. I wandered through the vast expanses of untouched wilderness, feeling both insignificant and alive in equal measure. Iceland felt like the answer to my health for a while. In Iceland I met many great people including Thórir, who was a member of the search and rescue team that went to the assistance of the crew of the US Navy Douglas C-117D (commonly mistaken for a DC-3) that wrecked onto the vast black sands of Sólheimasandur in 1973. Here's what he told me about how that place wreck got there: -

When the US Navy aircraft crashed in Iceland in 1973, I was part of the search and rescue team that responded to the call. I remember the day vividly - it was freezing and windy, but we knew we had to act fast. The plane had crashed due to icing in the carburettor, not because they had run out of fuel. The tanks were full and the crew had intentionally landed on the beach.

When we arrived at the scene, the crew had already been airlifted out by helicopter from the army base at Keflavík, so I never had a chance to meet them. As a rescue team member, I wasn't paid for the job. We did it in our free time out of a sense of duty and community.

The plane was mostly intact, but the Americans had already taken what they wanted - the motors, wings, and instruments. They spent two weeks collecting what they needed and then never came back. The canopy, nosecone, and tail were all still there. The plane has been lying there ever since, and it's hard to say who the owner is today. The farmer who owns the land where the plane crashed is, I suppose, now the owner.

The US Navy crew gave us the fuel left in the plane - several hundred litres of it. They fuel was in the wings, which is why they're nowhere to be seen now. I've yet to find them, but I know they're still out there somewhere. We used to fuel to power our snowmobiles for months.

Over the years, I've returned to the crash site several times, although less often than I used to. It's changed a lot since 1973. I took photos of the plane just after it crashed, and I've continued taking pictures ever since. I love to capture the beauty of Iceland - the northern lights are my favourite.

Suppose you visit the wool shop in Vík or the gift shop in Skógar. In that case, you can see Thórir's time-lapse videos on display and support his photography by buying a DVD or USB of his photos and videos of Iceland. I've visited that plane several times and it was actually my first 'target' in Iceland on my very first visit.

My heart brimmed with anticipation and a sense of adventure. Countless hours of research and browsing through amazing photographs had painted a picture of a mystical land rich in natural wonders. Among the many places that had captivated my imagination, the plane wreck at Sólheimasandur held a special allure. As a photographer passionate about aviation, the wreckage had become an emblem of mystery and intrigue. I yearned to stand before it, to capture its haunting beauty against the backdrop of the black sand beach. With my gear packed and a small Hyundai i10 as my trusty steed, I set off before dawn, navigating through the darkness and the treacherous driving conditions that the Icelandic weather can so often bestow upon the unwary traveller.

The wind howled relentlessly, and snowflakes whipped against the windshield, obscuring my view of the winding mountain passes leading out of Reykjavik. As I navigated the icy roadways, I clung to the wheel, my knuckles white with tension, determined not to let the challenging conditions deter me from my mission.

The blizzard raged as I ascended the mountain passes leading out of Reykjavík to the south coast, the world outside reduced to a white abyss. Each curve and turn tested my driving skills and resolve, but deep down, I knew the reward awaiting me on the other side would be worth every nerve-wracking moment.

As the first light of dawn began to pierce through the storm, a glimmer of hope ignited within me. The clouds parted, revealing a soft, ethereal glow that painted the landscape. I parked my car at the side of the road. Stepping out into the frigid air, I was immediately struck by the magnitude of the place.

Walking from Route 1, the Ring Road, towards the wreckage, my footsteps sank into the soft black sand, echoing in the stillness of the morning. The waves crashed against the shore, carrying a sense of ancient secrets whispered in the wind. The plane wreck sat stoically on the desolate shore, an enigmatic monument frozen in time. I couldn't help but wonder about the story behind this forsaken plane, how it had come to rest here, alone on this desolate beach.

As I drew nearer, my heart quickened with a mix of excitement and reverence. The skeletal remains of the aircraft towered before me, its broken parts reaching out like silent pleas for understanding. The years of exposure to the elements had taken their toll, transforming the metal into a canvas of rust and decay beneath the aluminium outer structure.

I couldn't help but feel a deep sense of awe and respect for this relic of the sky. It stood as a testament to the power of nature, the fragility of human endeavours, and the enduring allure of the unknown. With each photograph I captured, I sought to encapsulate the essence of this place, to convey the emotions it stirred within me.

At that moment, I realised that Iceland was so much more than the sum of its famous landmarks. It was much more than stories of elves and hidden people. It was a land of stories and untold histories, where nature and human existence intertwined in a dance of beauty and vulnerability. And with each step I took, I felt a profound connection to this extraordinary island, as if I had stumbled upon a part of myself waiting to be discovered.

As I left the wreckage behind and ventured further into the Icelandic landscape, I carried a newfound appreciation for the stories hidden in the most unexpected corners of the world. My passion for Iceland had begun.

There's another search and rescue member I met years ago, this time active in his role I had always been drawn to the allure of adventure, and my Due North expedition to Iceland promised just that. Little did I know that this journey would lead me to an extraordinary encounter and forge a friendship that would forever leave its mark on my heart.

His name was Lexi, a vibrant Icelander with a spirit as fierce as the winds that swept across the rugged landscape. From the moment I met, his enthusiasm for his homeland was infectious. His expertise in understanding the Icelandic terrain and weather is unrivalled. He became my guide, confidante, and partner in exploration.

One fateful day, as the winds howled and the blizzards raged, Lexi proposed an audacious plan. He wanted to take me to a place few had ever seen—the Langjökull glacier. With his unwavering determination, he arranged for a tracked snowcat to transport us through the treacherous terrain, braving the elements that concealed the secrets of the glacier.

As we embarked on our daring adventure in an old Swedish Snow Cat, I marvelled at the sheer power of nature. The blizzard whipped around us, obscuring our vision to mere meters ahead. The world became a monochromatic blur, a symphony of white and grey, but Lexi's unwavering spirit and unparalleled skill led us forward.

Guided by his intuition and an unwavering sense of direction, we ventured deeper into the glacier's heart. Finally, as if by some divine intervention, the storm momentarily abated, unveiling a sight that took my breath away—a newly discovered ice cave, vast and majestic.

The ice glimmered with an otherworldly beauty inside the cave, its icy walls casting a soft blue hue. Lexi's eyes sparkled with joy as we explored its depths, the size of a cathedral, our footsteps echoing in the silence. It was a moment of pure magic, a testament to the resilience and beauty of the natural world.

Knowing my passion for photography, Lexi had a surprise in store for me. He introduced me to his new boat, Sjöfn, named after the Norse goddess of love. His request was simple yet thrilling—he wanted me to capture the vessel in action for their website and social media.

Dressed in a dry suit, braving the frigid waters of Reykjavik Bay, shouting "man overboard" as I took the plunge as if I was being incredibly comedic and original, I immersed myself in the icy embrace of the sea. The freezing waves crashed around me, but my determination to capture the perfect shot eclipsed discomfort. Clutching my camera encased in a waterproof dome, I positioned myself as the boat circled me, capturing the essence of Sjöfn in her element.

As the boat glided back and forth, cutting through the choppy waters, I felt a sense of exhilaration. The sheer force of nature, the relentless winds and the biting cold became the backdrop to a symphony of moments frozen in time.

As I look back on that remarkable journey, I am reminded that life's greatest treasures often lie hidden beneath the rough surface. Through the blizzards and the freezing waters, I discovered the untamed wonders of Iceland and the enduring power of human connection. And for that, I will forever be grateful to Lexi, my guide, companion, and cherished friend.

I ventured further on my journey and Norway beckoned me with its own siren song. Norway always greeted me with majestic fjords that sliced through the land, creating a beautiful symphony of nature's grandeur. The quaint coastal villages nestled between towering mountains felt like scenes from a fairytale. The people I encountered embraced me with warmth and kindness, making me believe that perhaps, just maybe, I had found my place. The ethereal beauty of the Lofoten Islands stole my heart, its serene charm etching itself onto my soul. But even amidst this paradise, hiraeth whispered in my ear, reminding me that my journey wasn't over yet.

As I stood on the shores of Norway, torn between two lands that felt like home, I realised that health was both a blessing and a curse. It allowed me to see the beauty in every corner of the world but also left me with an insatiable yearning for a place that could never be found. I craved a place where I could bask in the glow of the midnight sun and dance under the Northern Lights. I longed for a home that combined the raw majesty of Iceland and the enchanting allure of Norway. One of the most insane experiences I've had in Norway is one that encouraged my decision to consider it a contender in my quest to find 'home.'

A feeling of solitude washed over me as I stood alone on the bridge spanning the rugged shores of Hamnøy and Sakrosøy, in the heart of the captivating Lofoten Islands. The COVID pandemic had cast its long shadow over the world, and here I was, alone, witnessing an incredible geomagnetic substorm performing a stunning dance in light amidst the vast expanse of nature. It was a rare moment of serenity, devoid of the usual throngs of photographers that often flocked to this "Instagram famous" location.

I couldn't help but feel a sense of awe and insignificance beneath this celestial spectacle. The vibrant green and purple dancing ribbons filled the sky as if a cosmic painter had splashed their palette across the heavens. My camera clicked incessantly, capturing the essence of the ethereal display, each shot a testament to the wonders of the universe.

This solitary communion with nature and the tranquillity of the moment was abruptly shattered by a voice that echoed across the bridge. "Holy shit, motherfucker!"

bellowed a local man named Odd-Petter, seemingly in response to the majesty of the aurora. Startled and disappointed that I was no longer alone, I turned towards the source of the exclamation, my eyes meeting his.

Odd-Petter, with his unruly beard and sparkling eyes, exuded a contagious energy that matched the fervour of the northern lights. There was an instant connection as if fate had orchestrated this encounter to bring two wanderers together in the vastness of Lofoten.

We exchanged enthusiastic greetings, our shared excitement evident in our voices. Odd-Petter explained that he was an aurora guide with no guests because fo the pandemic and he had come out alone, drawn to the same breathtaking spectacle that had captured my attention. At that moment, I knew our paths had crossed for a reason. Together, we embarked on a night of exploration and camaraderie.

We ventured towards the beautiful Reine area, our spirits soaring as we marvelled at the untouched beauty of the fjords and majestic peaks. With each step, our connection deepened, and the conversations flowed effortlessly, blending tales of travel, dreams, and the unique charm of Lofoten.

A distant light caught my attention as we wandered through the ethereal landscape. It was Ola, perched atop Reinebringen, a mountain that overlooked the picturesque village of Reine. We signalled to him with a flashlight, a beacon of friendship amidst the vast darkness. In those fleeting hours, I felt a profound sense of belonging. The bond forged between strangers amidst the celestial dance of the aurora had transcended the limits of time and distance. Lofoten, with its raw magnificence and the warmth of its people, had stirred something profound within me, a longing for a place to call home.

As the night passed, we bid farewell, knowing that our paths may diverge once more but forever, carrying the memories of that unforgettable night in our hearts. Lofoten had left an indelible mark, igniting a flame of possibility within me.

As I stood alone once again, gazing at the fading lights in the sky, I pondered the idea of calling Lofoten home. Its wild beauty, the serendipitous encounters, and the sense of community I had experienced beckoned me to explore this possibility further. Perhaps, amidst the rugged landscapes and the vibrant auroras, I would find not only a place to capture with my camera but a place where my restless soul could find solace and connection.

I returned with Kofifernweh and in these Due North adventures the days turned into weeks, and weeks turned into months as I immersed myself in the rhythm of life in Lofoten. I delved deeper into its soul-stirring landscapes, capturing moments of raw beauty that whispered stories untold. The enchanting archipelago became my muse, and every corner awaited a new adventure.

Odd-Petter and Ola became more than friends; they became my anchors in this newfound home. Their laughter and camaraderie infused my days with a sense of belonging I had long yearned for. Together, we ventured to the hidden gems of Lofoten and savoured the simplicity of life by the sea.

In the quiet evenings, as the sky transformed into a canvas painted with hues of pink and gold, waiting for Lady Aurora to put in an appearance, I would sit by the shoreline, my camera at my side, capturing the gentle dance of the waves. The serenity of those moments allowed me to reflect on the transformative power of this place and how it had touched my soul.

Lofoten had a way of evoking emotions transcending the mere act of photography. It was as if the very essence of the islands permeated my being, reminding me of the impermanence of life and the importance of embracing the present moment.

In the depths of winter, as the Arctic winds howled and snowflakes fell gently from the heavens, Lofoten revealed a different kind of magic. And in those moments of quiet reverence, I knew I had found my place in the world. The decision to call Lofoten home became more apparent with each passing day. The ever-changing landscape, the warmth of its people, and the profound sense of connection I felt were the pillars upon which my decision stood. Lofoten had woven its way into the fabric of my being, and I knew that I had become a part of its tapestry.

As I reflect on my journey, I am reminded that home is not simply a physical place but a feeling—a sense of belonging, of being seen and understood. Lofoten had become my sanctuary, a place where my passion for photography melded seamlessly with the untamed beauty of nature.

With its awe-inspiring landscapes and the unexpected friendships it has gifted me, Lofoten has become the chapter of my life that I never knew I needed. It is here, amidst the timeless beauty of these islands, that I have found my true north, my heart anchored by the majestic allure of Lofoten's shores.

In the end, I had to make a choice. I had to surrender to the reality that I could not claim the entire world as my home. With a heavy heart, I made the decision to settle in Norway. Its rugged beauty, welcoming people, and the faint echoes of hiraeth that resonated within its fjords made it the closest thing to a true home I had known since childhood.

But even now, as I sit in my cosy cabin on wheels waiting to once again overlook the Norwegian fjords, I feel a part of me yearning for the untamed wilderness of Iceland. Even though I have chosen Norway as my base, I have repeatedly been drawn back to Iceland. Its magnetic pull tugs at my heart, urging me to return and immerse myself again in its untamed beauty. I am irresistibly drawn to the cascading waterfalls, the black sand beaches, and the otherworldly landscapes that have become etched in my memory. I know that Hiraeth will forever be a companion on my journey, reminding me of the vastness of the world and the impossibility of capturing it all in one place. Yet, I am grateful for this unyielding longing, for it has opened my eyes to our planet's boundless wonders and made me appreciate the fleeting moments of belonging I find in every corner of the world.

Hiraeth, in its paradoxical nature, continues to fuel my wanderlust. It drives me to explore new lands, seek out hidden gems, and capture the essence of each place I encounter. It reminds me that home is not a fixed point on a map but a state of being, a feeling that transcends physical boundaries.

During my travels, I realised that hiraeth is more comprehensive than just a single place or culture. It is a universal longing shared by people from all walks of life. The nostalgia for a place we have never been and the ache for a sense of belonging elude us. And as a travel photographer, I am fortunate enough to witness this yearning reflected in the eyes of those I meet along my journeys.

Through my lens, I have captured the homesickness of a weary traveller gazing out of a train window, the wistful smiles of locals sharing stories of their homeland, and the shared sense of longing in the eyes of fellow adventurers searching for a place to call their own. I have come to understand that hiraeth is not a burden to bear alone but a shared human experience that binds us. I continue to explore the world with an open heart and an insatiable curiosity. I have learned to embrace the transient nature of my existence, finding solace in the knowledge that home can be located in fleeting moments, connections forged with kindred spirits, and the memories I carry within me.

And so, as I wander through the world, capturing fragments of its soul with my camera, I embrace the bittersweet dance of hiraeth. It guides me towards moments of connection and places that feel like home, even if only briefly. And in the depths of my being, I know that I am blessed to have many places to call home. Yet, I am forever bound to the longing for a place that exists beyond the boundaries of geography—a place that resides within the recesses of my restless spirit.

For now, I will continue to chase the elusive magic of hiraeth, knowing that as long as my heart remains open, I will find glimpses of home in every corner of the world. Ultimately, home is not confined to a specific latitude or longitude. It is not a mere arrangement of bricks and mortar but a feeling that resides within our hearts. Home is the warmth that embraces us, the connections that uplift us, and the sense of belonging that transcends borders. It is in the embrace of loved ones, the shared laughter, and the moments of quiet contentment. And as I continue my journey, I carry with me the profound realization that home is not a destination to be reached but a state of being that we have within us, wherever we may roam. Home is not a place. It's a feeling.

CHAPTER 6
SAMBA

Celebration And Joy

Rio de Janeiro, the city of Carnival, samba, and caipirinhas, is a vibrant and colourful city on Brazil's Atlantic coast. I arrived in Rio before the time of my beloved van, Kofifernweh, but with an open mind and a thirst for adventure. As soon as I arrived, I was swept up in the energy of the city, which was palpable and infectious.

One of the first things I did in Rio was walk along the world-famous Copacabana beach. The beach is a long stretch of white sand and clear blue waters, and it is bordered by high-rise buildings and luxury hotels. I watched as people sunbathed, played beach volleyball, and went for a swim. The atmosphere was alive, and the people enjoyed life to the fullest. It was like there was a party, but there wasn't. This was not normal to me. My life at this point was very systematic and ordered. Rio was a stark contrast to me. A few moments of unease reared up, but I reminded myself each time that it's essential to engage in activities that challenge our everyday routines and push us outside of our comfort zones. Juxtaposing our daily life with new experiences and perspectives can lead to profound insights and personal growth. It forces us to confront the unexpected and challenges our assumptions, leading us to new ideas and perspectives. There's a delicate balance involved in maximising juxtaposition to push our creativity. Still, it's about the art of simultaneously creating harmony and tension. When we step outside our usual way of thinking, we open ourselves up to new possibilities and a more nuanced understanding of the world around us.

We should embrace chaos and unpredictability in our lives. Doing things that juxtapose our everyday life can be a way to introduce chaos into our routines and break free from limiting patterns of thought and behaviour. By challenging ourselves to try new things, we can cultivate creativity, resilience, and adaptability, all essential for personal growth and fulfilment. Ultimately, engaging in activities outside our usual way of thinking can help us lead more meaningful and fulfilling lives by broadening our horizons and enriching our understanding of ourselves and the world. I'm sure we've all heard the quote that says the definition of insanity is to do the same thing time after time and expect different results. If you do what you've always done, you'll get what you've always gotten. If you want something you've never had, you must be willing to do something you've never done. Ultimately, we can't become what we need to be by remaining what we are, right? Right. So, Rio would juxtapose all my Arctic adventures, and I would experience new things, including Brazilian barbecue (which I was very excited about!)

I decided to hike up through the lush rainforest to a cave at the top of a mountain in Tijuca National Park. The hike was challenging, and I struggled to keep up with the locals, who seemed to have boundless energy. Along the trail, the incline was demanding. Tree roots were the ever-present trip hazard, and as sweat poured off my brow, monkeys humped in the canopy overhead. Hiking in a rainforest is an immersive experience that engages all your senses. The lush greenery, the fragrant air, and the sounds of the forest surround you as you make your way through the dense vegetation. The overhead canopy blocks sunlight, trapping moisture and creating a humid environment. The rainforest floor is often wet and muddy underfoot. The trail at Tijuca winds through tall trees, thick vines, and dense undergrowth, with occasional glimpses of small streams and waterfalls. As you walk, you hear the sounds of birds chirping, insects buzzing, and the rustling of leaves and branches. As well as the monkeys, you encounter other wildlife, such as sloths, snakes and colourful birds. The rainforest is teeming with life, and every step along the trail brings new discoveries. The rainforest juxtaposes the city that sits in the foothills beneath.

As the hike progressed, I encountered challenges such as steep inclines, slippery slopes, and narrow paths. Still, the reward was the stunning beauty of the rainforest, which seemed to go on forever, followed by the view I wanted of the city in the direction of the Sugar Loaf mountain seen from inside a large cavern. The bay, the ocean, the tree canopy, and even helicopters flying beneath me were all in that one frame. The hike was a test of endurance, but it was also an unforgettable experience that will stay with me as it has long after I left the forest. But the reward was worth it. I sat there for a while, taking it all in and feeling grateful for the opportunity to experience such a beautiful place.

Another unforgettable experience in Rio was sailing in the bay past Sugarloaf Mountain. The Sugarloaf Mountain is a peak that rises 396 metres above the harbour and is one of Rio's most famous landmarks. The view of the mountain from the bay is stunning, and it is something that I will never forget. The bay is also home to many islands and secluded beaches, and we could stop at some of these to swim and explore.

One of the highlights of my trip to Rio was taking a "doors off" helicopter flight over the city. If there's one piece of advice I can give about sightseeing flights, you should always take the "doors off" option! Not only does it allow you to get the iconic Instagram shot of your feet hanging in mid-air like I did directly over the Christ the Redeemer statue, but it is also an experience that makes you feel much more connected to the scenery below. The flight was an exhilarating experience, giving me a unique perspective of the city. From high above, I could see the sprawling favelas I'd explored on foot, home to many of the city's inhabitants. Despite the poverty and hardship that many of the people living in these areas face, there was a sense of joy and celebration that permeated the city.

The lesson I learned from my time in Rio is the spirit of "Samba". Sambe is a Portuguese word that refers to the joy and celebration prevalent in Brazil. Despite many people's challenges, they can find (and make) joy and happiness in their lives. I was inspired by the resilience and determination of the people of Rio, and it taught me the importance of finding joy amid arduous circumstances. Happiness is a choice. It isn't something that's ready-made; it's something that comes from a conscious choice. Nothing will make you happy until you choose happiness. Ultimately, happiness will not come to you but from you. You can't rely on someone else to make you happy. It's all in you. Samba is joy and celebration. Life is a samba. It's a never-ending dance of joy and love. Live it to the fullest.

I left Rio with a renewed sense of purpose and a greater appreciation for life. The city and its people taught me that no matter where we come from or our circumstances, we all have the capacity for joy and celebration. The only other place I felt a vibe that was anything like this was in Havana, Cuba. I stayed in one of the local's homes, getting a raw experience of their optimism and the celebration of the little that they have in this communist state.

When I arrived in Havana, I was immediately enveloped by the vibrant energy and happy spirit that permeated the city. It was as if the rhythm of salsa music filled the air, intermingling with the laughter and chatter of the locals. Havana felt alive with a palpable sense of joy, exuding an infectious and captivating charm.

Exploring the bustling streets, I couldn't help but notice the stark contrast between Havana and my hometown of London. The infrastructure had a rustic charm, showcasing a blend of faded grandeur and vibrant colours. The historic buildings, adorned with intricate balconies and ornate facades, seemed to narrate tales of a bygone era. In contrast to London's sleek and modern architecture, Havana's charm lay in its weathered beauty, as if each crack and peeling paint told a story of resilience and history. One of the most fascinating aspects of Havana was its time capsule of classic cars that graced the streets. As I strolled along the avenues, I was surrounded by a mesmerising array of vintage dinosaur automobiles, each a testament to Cuba's enduring spirit. These colourful relics from the past, lovingly maintained and passed down through generations, added a sense of nostalgia and charm to the cityscape. From vibrant convertibles to sleek sedans, the streets of Havana became a living museum of automotive history. It was as if I had entered a bygone era, where these beautifully preserved cars told stories of resilience and resourcefulness. In a world dominated by modern models, Havana's classic cars stood as a symbol of Cuba's ability to make the most of what it had, a testament to the ingenuity and pride of its people.

What struck me most was the difference in connectedness between the two cities. In London, technology permeated every aspect of life, with people constantly engrossed in their smartphones, absorbed in their virtual worlds. But in Havana, I witnessed a refreshing absence of screens and distractions. Instead, the streets were filled with people engaged in lively conversations, their genuine warmth and openness radiating through every interaction. A true sense of community, of human connection, transcended the digital divide.

In Havana, time seemed to move at its own pace, free from modern life's relentless rush and urgency. The lack of constant connectivity allowed people to be fully present, savouring the simple pleasures and embracing the joy of human connection. It was a gentle reminder that, amidst the allure of technological advancements, the essence of life lies in the moments shared with others, the laughter, and the genuine connections formed.

As I immersed myself in the vibrant tapestry of Havana's streets, I couldn't help but be captivated by the city's spirit. With its lively charm and warm-hearted people, Havana left an everlasting mark on my soul, a testament to the richness of human experience found within the streets of this enchanting city. It was a reminder to embrace the beauty of imperfections, prioritise human connection over constant virtual engagement, and cherish life's simple joys, just as the spirit of sambe encourages. Finding happiness involves releasing preconceived notions of how your life should unfold and embracing it for its unique beauty. The most remarkable experiences are often found in the simplicity of everyday moments, and only those with wisdom can fully appreciate them. True happiness lies not in obtaining everything you desire but in developing a genuine appreciation for what you already possess.

CHAPTER 7
KEYIF

A Sense Of Contentment, Pleasure And Relaxation

Keyif is a Turkish word that translates to a state of calm pleasure, relaxation, and contentment. It's a feeling I experienced during my travels through central Turkey, particularly in the town of Göreme and the surrounding region of Cappadocia. This unique landscape is known for its fairy chimneys, underground cities, and hot air balloons that fill the skies at sunrise, creating a serene and surreal atmosphere.

I arrived in Göreme early in the morning after an overnight drive from Istanbul, eager to witness the sunrise and the hot air balloons that float above the unique rock formations. I was not disappointed. I decided to hike up to one of the viewpoints overlooking the town, where I sat and watched the balloons for hours, feeling a sense of peace and contentment wash over me. As the sun began to rise, the sky was painted with pink, orange, and yellow hues, and the sound of the burners firing up filled the silence. The balloons slowly lifted off the ground, and the sky was soon filled with colourful orbs floating majestically in the air. The morning's quiet stillness, the gentle rustling of the wind, and the beauty of the balloons against the sunrise backdrop created an atmosphere of pure Keyif. I took one photo of the balloons at sunrise from inside a cave. The photograph captures a breathtaking moment at the break of dawn. The image frames a stunning view of the surreal landscape as hot air balloons gracefully ascend into the sky, painting it with vibrant hues against the soft, golden glow of the rising sun.

From the vantage point inside a cave, the photo offers a unique perspective, immersing the viewer in the ancient geological wonders of the region. Weathered and textured cave walls provide a frame that adds depth and a sense of mystery to the scene. It's as if the observer is granted a glimpse into a hidden sanctuary, a secret realm where nature's splendour unfolds. As the hot air balloons ascend, their vibrant colours stand out against the canvas of the sky. Shades of rich reds, oranges, and yellows blend harmoniously with the serene hazy backdrop, creating a captivating visual symphony. Like delicate orbs of dreams, the balloons seem to float effortlessly, suspended between earth and sky as if defying gravity.

The soft morning light casts a warm glow on the landscape, revealing the unique rock formations of Cappadocia. The distinctive fairy chimneys, sculpted by the hands of time, emerge as silent witnesses to centuries of history and culture. Their whimsical shapes starkly contrast with the sky's vastness, creating a captivating interplay between the earthly and the celestial.

In this ethereal moment, the photograph captures the sheer beauty of the hot air balloons against the backdrop of Cappadocia and the sense of tranquillity and awe that the experience evokes. It symbolises the freedom of flight, the sense of adventure, and the beauty of embracing the unknown. The image speaks to the imagination and invites contemplation. It encapsulates the wonder of witnessing the world from a different perspective, from soaring above the earth and gazing upon its natural wonders. It reminds us of the boundless possibilities that lie beyond the horizon, urging us to embrace the extraordinary and seek moments of beauty and serenity in our lives.

In this photograph of hot air balloons at sunrise, taken from the shelter of a cave, the viewer is transported to a place where the realms of nature and human ingenuity converge. It serves as a reminder of the power of exploration, the enchantment of witnessing the world's wonders, and the sheer beauty that awaits those who dare to step outside their comfort zones.

Over the next few days, I explored the region surrounding Cappadocia, visiting underground cities, hiking through the valleys, photographing the blood moon against a cliff house, and taking in the unique landscape and culture. One of the most memorable experiences was staying in a cave hotel, which was carved into the soft rock formations. The cool interior of the cave was a welcome relief from the hot sun outside, and the unique ambience of the hotel added to the feeling of Keyif.

The concept of Keyif is deeply ingrained in Turkish culture. It extends beyond the simple pleasure of relaxing and enjoying the moment. It's a way of life that emphasises the importance of taking the time to appreciate the simple things, find joy in the present moment, and cultivate a sense of contentment and gratitude. This way of life is evident in the warmth and hospitality of the Turkish people, who welcome visitors with open arms and share their culture and traditions with pride. One particular memory of this was sitting in a café enjoying a spectacular Turkish coffee. I was the only customer at the time, and I was busy doing my coffee photo for a deal I had with Lonely Planet when the owner's puppy came and sat with me. The puppy was tiny – literally the same size as my DSLR camera. Rather than chew or play as would be expected of a puppy, the little dog just sat there, apparently very relaxed and content to be in my company.

Dogs have a unique ability to find contentment in life without any possessions. Contentment is, as the puppy showed, not a possession to be prized; instead, it's a quality of thought and a state of mind. Unlike humans, dogs are not concerned with material possessions or accumulating wealth. They are content with the simple things in life, such as food, water, and love. Dogs find joy in the little things, like walking with their owners, playing fetch, or even lying in the sun. They do not need expensive toys or designer clothes to be happy. In fact, they are often more content with a stick or a ball than with any expensive toy. Perhaps this is one of the reasons why dogs are such beloved pets. They teach us that happiness is not about what we have but how we live our lives. They remind us to find joy in the simple things and to appreciate the love and companionship of those around us. So next time you see a happy dog wagging its tail, perhaps coming to sit with you in a café in Göreme, take a moment to appreciate the contentment that comes from a life lived without possessions.

As I reflect on my time in central Turkey, I realise that the experience was about more than just the beauty of the landscape or the thrill of the hot air balloons filling the skies at dawn. It was about embracing the concept of Keyif and taking the time to appreciate the small moments of beauty and joy in life. It's a lesson that I carry with me in my travels and everyday life, reminding me to slow down, take a deep breath, and savour life's simple pleasures.

The experience of being surrounded by hot air balloons at sunrise in Cappadocia was indeed a once-in-a-lifetime experience. Still, it also taught me a valuable lesson about the importance of finding joy and contentment in the present moment. It's a lesson I carry with me as I continue my travels, seeking out new experiences and discovering the beauty and richness of the world around me. From a moment on my second morning, whilst sitting on the roof of my cave hotel, I came up with the motto that I live by and offer others to follow. Once in a lifetime, as often as you can. You'll see it pop up a few times in this book. Well, it had to fit into the Turkey chapter because that's where it was born, so here's what it means to me:

The phrase 'once in a lifetime as often as you can' is all about living life to the fullest and making the most of every opportunity that comes your way. It encourages individuals to take advantage of unique experiences and try new things because they may only occasionally come around. Just as there's a first time for everything, there's also a last. We don't know when our 'last' will be, so we should maximise our opportunities. If we want to do something, but the option isn't necessarily given to us, I have a phrase in ink on my left shoulder that may help. It says, 'Find a way or make one.'

The concept behind this phrase is that we should approach life with a sense of adventure and excitement and make the most of every moment. We should actively seek out these opportunities and embrace them whenever possible.

While some experiences may indeed be once-in-a-lifetime, other opportunities often come close or as memorable. Living our lives with an open mind and willingness to explore new opportunities allows us to create our own 'once-in-a-lifetime' moments and memories. In essence, the phrase encourages us to seize the day and live life to the fullest with a sense of wonder and appreciation for all the world has to offer. If we follow this guiding principle, achieving keyif will undoubtedly accompany it.

CHAPTER 8
SERENDIPITY

The Occurrence Of Unexpected And Fortunate Discoveries Or Events By Chance

During several journeys through Morocco's vibrant and enchanting land, little did I know the twists of serendipity that awaited me. They say travel is a gateway to unexpected encounters and delightful surprises, and my adventure would prove to be no exception. Amidst the challenges and unforeseen detours, I would come to appreciate the magical dance of serendipity, where strange or seemingly bad things hold hidden blessings. A captivating scene unfolds in the bustling streets of Marrakech amidst the vibrant tapestry of colours and scents. A photograph captures the essence of this moment – one of my favourite photos from Morocco. A Berber figure standing stooped, clad in a flowing gown adorned in shades of blue and grey. His hood is drawn up, hiding his face, leaving an air of mystery and intrigue.

In the heart of this enchanting image, the Berber holds a large, rusty key in his weathered hands. The key, worn with age and history, carries the weight of stories untold. Its jagged teeth bear witness to the countless times it has turned within ancient locks, unlocking secrets from the depths of time.

Before the figure, recessed in the ochre walls, stands an old wooden door, weathered by the passage of years. The wood, etched with intricate patterns and marked by the touch of time, bears the scars of countless journeys and countless tales. Its texture tells of stories woven into the fabric of the city, tales of joy and sorrow, triumphs and challenges.

In this evocative moment frozen in time by my camera, the Berber gently inserts the key into the enormous lock. The symbolism of this act is palpable—a connection between past and present, an unlocking of possibilities and hidden treasures. The door creaks open as the key turns within the lock, revealing a world of mystery and wonder beyond.

The scene is filled with contrasts—the ancient, contemporary, worn, and vibrant. It serves as a poignant reminder of the rich tapestry of history woven within the bustling streets of Marrakech. It speaks of the Berber's deep connection to their cultural heritage, their guardianship of traditions passed down through generations.

Amidst the emotional chaos of the city, the Berber figure stands as a testament to the resilience and the power of the human spirit. Their presence hints at the stories they carry within, the wisdom gained from navigating the labyrinthine alleys and embracing the city's ever-changing landscape. They embody the spirit of Marrakech, a city where ancient traditions coexist with the pulse of modern life.

As I gaze now upon this captivating photograph, I'm invited to step into the world it encapsulates. I'm reminded of the power of a single key, capable of unlocking the doors of my own destiny. I'm transported to the streets of Marrakech, where history and culture intertwine, the past and present converge in a symphony of colours, and the allure of the unknown beckons us to explore. Morocco's tapestry of colours, scents, and ancient traditions beckoned me with its charm. From the bustling markets of Marrakech to the serene Atlas Mountains, I traversed its landscapes with an eager heart and a backpack filled with dreams (and camera gear). However, the path I envisioned quickly unravelled, revealing a mosaic of unusual circumstances and peculiar happenings that would forever shape my journey.

The scorching sun bore down relentlessly, testing my endurance as I ventured through the maze-like streets of Essaouira. The heat seemed oppressive, and my weary feet whispered tales of discomfort and struggle. Yet, serendipity stepped in in the face of these challenges, weaving its magic. It led me to stumble upon hidden riads with welcoming courtyards, where I found respite and encountered kind souls who shared their stories and wisdom over glasses of fresh mint tea.

Seeking solace from the relentless heat, I embarked on a voyage to the majestic Sahara Desert. The shifting dunes stretched endlessly before me, a canvas of golden sands. In the solitude of that vast expanse, serendipity manifested itself once more. Amidst the tranquillity, I chanced upon Berber who welcomed me into their fold, inviting me to partake in their traditions and savour the simplicity of desert life. Their hospitality and resilience in harsh conditions reminded me that sometimes, unexpected detours lead us to the most extraordinary experiences.

But serendipity bestowed upon me a genuinely remarkable encounter during my exploration of the remote Moroccan countryside. As I ventured through rocky hills and valleys, a peculiar sight emerged. Nestled amidst the arid landscape, a solitary tree stood defiantly, its branches adorned with many goats. They clung to the branches with remarkable agility, munching on leaves like they had defied gravity.

Mesmerised by this surreal spectacle, I approached the tree, captivated by the peculiar beauty. A local shepherd, with a smile that mirrored the whimsy of serendipity, shared the tale behind this enchanting sight. The goats, driven by a natural instinct to survive, had discovered that the tree's leaves provided sustenance in this barren land. Through the whimsical dance of serendipity, they found a source of nourishment that defied conventional wisdom.

This encounter became a guiding metaphor for my own journey. It taught me to embrace the unexpected and find solace in uncertainty. The hardships I encountered were not stumbling blocks but serendipitous detours leading to extraordinary encounters and personal growth. Serendipity, the art of finding hidden blessings in seemingly strange or challenging circumstances, had become my faithful companion.

As I continued to navigate Morocco, I embraced the whims of serendipity with an open heart. The arduous journey from one part of the country to another allowed me to connect with fellow travellers, each carrying their own tales of serendipity and the unexpected turns that enriched their lives. The bustling markets transformed into treasure troves of delightful surprises, where chance encounters led to incredible adventures.

I invite you to embrace the beauty of serendipity in your own journey. Allow yourself to be open to life's unforeseen twists and turns. For amidst the challenges and unexpected moments lie hidden gems of joy, growth, and self-discovery. Embrace the moments when serendipity knocks on your door, for it is in those instances that the testing trials of life become unforgettable experiences.

As I reflect on my time in Morocco, I am reminded that serendipity reminds us that our misfortunes or strange encounters hold a deeper purpose. It nudges us to release our grip on control and surrender to the flow of life, trusting that the universe has a grand design far beyond our understanding. The challenges and surprises we encounter along the way are not random occurrences but threads intricately woven into the fabric of our personal narratives.

So, remember that serendipity may be at play when faced with adversity or unexpected twists. During these moments, we are invited to trust, to let go of our preconceived notions, and to embrace the unknown with curiosity and an open heart. For in those moments, we may stumble upon the experiences that shape us and lead us closer to our true selves. As you set forth on your own journey through foreign lands or simply your daily life. Embrace serendipity as your faithful companion, knowing that the strange or unexpected moments hold the potential for growth, connection, and transformative experiences. And may you discover, as I have, that the beauty of serendipity lies not only in the destination but in the very act of embracing the journey itself.

As I bid farewell to the enchanting land of Morocco, I carry with me the lessons of serendipity. Its dance has imprinted upon my soul the beauty of embracing the unexpected, finding joy in challenges, and recognising that the extraordinary often hides in the most unlikely places.

Here's the caveat: Serendipitous moments aren't always immediately positive, as I learned from the 'warm up' trip that preceded Due North II. As I embarked on a journey through the enchanting landscapes of Scotland, little did I know that the hand of serendipity would reveal itself in a rather unexpected and challenging manner. It was a dark and rainy evening when I was in a remote area devoid of phone data connection, far from the bustling city lights. The tranquillity of the surroundings was shattered by a sudden burst of the van's tyre as it collided with an unseen rock hiding in the grass in the gravel parking area.

At that moment, the veil of serendipity took on a different guise. What seemed like a stroke of misfortune became an opportunity to test my resilience and adaptability. With the rain pouring down relentlessly, I gathered my courage and embarked on the task of changing the tyre. Rolling on the wet ground under the van, feeling the cold puddles seeping through my clothes, I wrestled with the lug nuts and the challenges the dark presented.

During the arduous and uncomfortable experience, I couldn't help but contemplate the deeper meaning behind it all. Serendipity, I realised, does not always come wrapped in the garb of positivity. It can test us, push us to our limits, and challenge our perception of what is favourable. Through these moments of adversity and discomfort, the true strength of character emerges.

As I finally tightened the last lug nut and rose to my feet, soaked and weary in the dark, I couldn't help but feel a sense of accomplishment. The experience taught me that positive or seemingly negative serendipity holds transformative power. It reveals our resilience, capacity to adapt, and the hidden strengths that lie dormant within us. Unfortunately, it also taught me the price of a new all-terrain tyre in the middle of nowhere.

In the solitude of that dark Scottish night, I embraced the understanding that serendipity is not always a gentle breeze guiding us towards pleasant surprises. It can also be a storm that tests our mettle and reshapes our perspective. In those moments of struggle and challenge, we find the opportunity to grow, discover our own depths of perseverance, and emerge stronger and wiser.

As I continued my journey through the mystical landscapes of Scotland, the tyre change became a symbolic milestone. Each subsequent encounter with serendipity, whether delightful or demanding, carried the resonance of that rainy night. I welcomed each twist of fate, knowing that there lay an opportunity for personal growth and resilience behind the veil of chance and happenstance.

When faced with moments that seem to test your resolve, remember that serendipity's touch can be as unpredictable as the Scottish weather. Embrace the challenges as opportunities to tap into your inner strength and fortitude. Through the seemingly tricky moments, the true beauty of serendipity emerges, reshaping us into individuals capable of weathering any storm. Life itself is serendipitous. It's a chance event that is mathematically as close to impossible as possible. Most people who could exist will never exist – it's a mathematical certainty. You are entirely against the odds merely in being here. You are very lucky to be alive. While driving inordinate distances, I have basically completed Spotify, so I often listen to the deeper meaning behind the music in my playlists. Here's one of my favourites: -

The line "I am the one thing in life I can control" from the musical Hamilton carries a powerful and profound message about personal agency and self-determination. It speaks to the concept that amidst the tumultuous and unpredictable circumstances of life, one's own thoughts, actions, and choices remain within control. Serendipitous moments come along and often please us, like being in the right place at the right time for a great photo in Morocco, but sometimes some moments are more testing, like the whole tyre situation in Scotland.

In the context of the character Alexander Hamilton's journey, this line reflects his unwavering determination and ambition to make a mark on the world. It underscores his belief that regardless of the external forces that shape his circumstances, he can shape his destiny through his actions and decisions.

On a broader level, this line resonates with the universal human experience. It emphasises the importance of taking responsibility for our lives, recognising our agency, and embracing the power to make a difference. It reminds us that while we may not have control over the events that unfold around us or the actions of others, we do possess the ability to shape our attitudes, responses, and choices.

Furthermore, this line highlights the significance of self-reliance and self-belief. It encourages individuals to trust their abilities, have faith in their capacity to overcome challenges and take ownership of their personal growth and development. It reminds us that our actions, values, and character can serve as steadfast anchors in a world that often feels beyond our control.

Ultimately, "I am the one thing in life I can control" is a powerful affirmation of human agency and resilience. It inspires individuals to seize the reins of their own lives, navigate the complexities of existence with determination and purpose, and find strength in the knowledge that, amidst uncertainties, they possess the capacity to shape their destinies. Honestly, go and listen to 'Wait for it' in which the line appears. And as for chapter title itself, serendipity is the magic of discovering something marvellous when you least expect it while pursuing something entirely different. The delightful happenstance, the unforeseen gift, brings a sprinkle of enchantment into our lives. Embrace the unpredictability of life and allow serendipity to lead you towards remarkable and extraordinary experiences.

CHAPTER 9
THE CALL OF THE WILD

The Primal Longing For Untamed Nature

The Canadian Rockies had always been on my bucket list. I had heard so much about the natural beauty of this place, and I was eager to explore it. So, when I got an opportunity to visit the Rockies during winter, I jumped at the chance. It was an adventure of a lifetime and one that left a lasting impression on me. The cold was biting, but the beauty of the landscape made it worth it. The Call of the Wild is a Canadian saying, and I don't need to explain the words themselves, but here's what it means to me. It's a potent force. It awakens our primal instincts, reminding us of our connection to the natural world. It's not just a desire to escape civilisation – it's a yearning to connect with something bigger than ourselves. Something that perhaps can't even be explained in itself. It's a force that can't be denied, leading us down paths we never thought possible and awakening our innermost desires. It's both a whisper in the ear of every adventurer, calling to explore new horizons, and a primal scream through our souls, reminding us of our place in the world, urging us to follow our passions and live our lives with both purpose and courage.

My journey began at the stunning Abraham Lake, completely frozen over. The sun rose early in the morning, casting a beautiful golden light across the landscape. Still, before that, I was tested by my senses. Still twilight, I put on my ice spikes and ventured onto the ice-covered lake to explore and choose where I'd set up my camera and tripod when that light finally came. There was a stiff winter breeze, with no sounds besides the moving air. That relative silence was broken by a wolf's distant, high-pitched howl. My excitement peaked as I realised that the bustle of Calgary was far behind me, and I was out in the true wilderness.

A few minutes passed, and I was still scouting the expansive frozen lake in search of the spot I wanted. Cracks created incredible leading lines, and the bubbles trapped in the ice were a perfect foreground. That howling wolf seemed to be getting louder, and I noticed some barks and yips fading behind it. I strained my eyes in the direction all this commotion was coming from and froze for a moment when I saw that the first wolf was on the ice, staring at me whilst zig-zagging in my direction with its nose appearing to lead the way. The rest of the pack, barking and yipping, were silhouetted against the snow-covered mountain slope they were running down, straight at me. Boy, was I glad I'd worn ice spikes! I ran (kinda) off the ice and back to my rental car as fast as I could, hopping the gap at the shoreline where the ice became slush as it broke with the currents lapping the shore. Never before had I felt like I was food. The wolves apparently didn't like the look of the car or the nearby road, the David Thompson Highway, and diverted from me. I waited 30 minutes and ventured out onto the ice again, this time joined by a local who was ice skating before heading to work. The methane ice bubbles that formed under the lake's frozen surface created a surreal and magical scene that I will never forget. I spent hours photographing the frozen lake and the surrounding peaks before moving on to Medicine Lake. I'll never forget the skater saying, "Hey, did you notice those wolves sat on the shore over there?"

Medicine Lake was another natural wonder that left me in awe. The lake was frozen, and the snow-covered trees created a beautiful contrast against the deep blue sky. This was the first time I had seen something like it. It was as if I had stepped into a magical wonderland, and I was glad to have my camera with me to capture the beauty of it all. I spotted a moose cow and her two young as I drove around the lake edge looking for the spot I wanted to shoot, but nothing else. Despite this, I felt constantly as if I were being watched. I couldn't place the feeling precisely, but I felt I wasn't alone that morning, and my eyes kept turning to the timber.

The road trip from Medicine Lake to Jasper was a scenic one. On the way, I encountered wildlife, such as elk and big-horn sheep, which was an unforgettable experience. The snow-capped mountains and frozen lakes were a sight to behold, and I felt like I was in a winter wonderland.

I drove along the Icefields Parkway, which is considered one of the most scenic drives in the world. The highway was lined with snow-covered trees and frozen lakes, and the towering mountains on all sides created a stunning backdrop. I stopped at Morant's Curve, a famous spot for photographing the iconic train that runs through the Canadian Rockies. The train was an impressive sight, and the snow-covered landscape provided a stunning contrast to the red and black of the train.

The trip was not without its challenges. The cold was intense, and my camera gear struggled to cope with the conditions. But the beauty of the Rockies made it all worth it. The trip also taught me the importance of being prepared for any eventuality. I learned to dress in layers, carry extra camera batteries, and keep my equipment warm to prevent it from freezing. My trip to the Canadian Rockies was an adventure of a lifetime. The beauty of the landscape, the wildlife, and the winter activities made it a trip I will never forget. The call of the wild is strong, and I am eager to explore more of the world's natural wonders.

This call to adventure and exploration can take many forms, from hiking and camping in remote wilderness areas to climbing mountains, kayaking down rivers, or simply spending time in quiet contemplation in a natural setting. For many, answering this call can be a transformative experience, bringing a renewed sense of purpose and meaning to our lives and connecting us to something greater than ourselves.

In the context of travel and photography, the call of the wild often inspires people to seek out remote and wild places and capture nature's beauty and majesty through their lens. It can also drive them to seek new experiences and challenges, whether hiking to a remote mountain summit, exploring a hidden canyon, or tracking elusive wildlife through dense forests and rugged terrain. Ultimately, the call of the wild is a powerful reminder of our connection to the natural world and the importance of preserving and protecting the wild places that inspire us to explore and experience the world in new and meaningful ways.

My trip to the Rockies was not quite over. I had to make the journey from Hinton to Calgary to catch my flight.

In my ever-present quest for adventure, I decided I wouldn't take the main roads. The fire within me told me to take the back roads, maybe some logging roads, and see things that not everybody gets to see. The drive was five hours and would take me down along the eastern foothills of the Rockies towards Nordegg and Rocky Mountain House before turning towards Calgary across the Alberta prairies. One of the stupid ideas I had (of which there are many) while driving here was to shoot a piece for social media about depth in the composition. I wanted to convey the idea that photos should have a foreground, middle ground and background in order to convey depth. Still, I wanted to do it uniquely. Photography isn't simply capturing an image but also telling a story through depth and composition. It's often depth that can capture a viewer's attention and draw them into the scene. I needed to make something that made this point. In my mind at the time, nothing was more unique than shooting an apparently never-ending, somewhat boring expanse of the area I was driving through. It was lovely to look at, but taking a good photo would have been tricky, making it the ideal location. My stupid idea was to take a big cardboard box and write the words "foreground interest" on it, making it the foreground of the photo. See, stupid. I pulled over, got my stupid cardboard box out of the car, and placed it in the middle of the road. I was far away from anything that could be called 'civilisation.' That feeling I had around Medicine Lake was with me again. I didn't feel alone.

I looked over to my right and saw tracks leading from the road up a gradient, ending at a ridgeline with some trees lining it. Over my right shoulder, the ridgeline continued and led to another copse. Both were evergreen, so they were dense and dark despite the season. Then, I realised those tracks were a little strange, and my focus went back to them.

They went up the steep slope in the snow leaving knee-deep holes. That's nothing out of the ordinary – a moose could do that. What a moose doesn't do is leave tracks about a metre and a half apart and have the perfect impression of a human foot, only about twice the size of mine and almost perfectly in line. The tracks weren't brand new – the sun was shining, and the sky was clear, so there was some 'softening' to the tracks as the snow melted and began to fill the holes and loosen the definition. I was in a place known throughout recent history to be the home of many sasquatch sightings. Here I was, staring at these tracks and realising that feeling. The more we learn, the more we realise we don't know. The unknown is a reminder that there is always something else. Something mysterious. Mystery creates wonder, and wonder is the basis of man's desire to understand.

Three years later, that feeling came back. Canada was a distant memory. This time, I found myself in Germany in Kofifernweh. I was near Berg Eltz Burg, a stunning medieval castle nestled in western Germany's hills above the Moselle River. The castle dates back to the 12th century. It has been owned by the same family for over 850 years, making it one of the few castles in Germany to have never been destroyed or changed hands.

The castle is surrounded by dense forests and is situated in a small valley, which adds to its mystique and charm. This is why I was here – I wanted to capture this impressive sight at sunrise, so I parked nearby to be ready for the early rise. As you approach Burg Eltz, you are met with a fantastic view - a tall, stone fortress with turrets and towers rising above the trees. It's not as 'Disney' as

Neuschwanstein Castle, but it isn't far off. The castle is accessible only by foot and requires a short hike through the forest, which adds to the sense of adventure and discovery. I'm sure it would've been a great photo, but it didn't happen. Here's why:

I was parked Kofifernweh in a car park surrounded by steep slopes and thick trees in the forest. I had driven a few kilometres from the nearest civilisation to find a spot where I could rest and be one with nature, ideally for the morning hike. At first, everything seemed serene. The sound of crickets and frogs filled the air as I enjoyed the cool breeze blowing through my open windows after the hot day. However, it took only a short time for things to take a turn. Suddenly, I heard noises in the forest, breaking branches and rustling leaves. I assumed it was just the local wildlife and continued listening. But as the sounds grew louder, my unease increased. Without warning, all the sounds stopped. No frogs, crickets, wind rustling leaves in branches, nor snapping twigs. It was eerily silent, and I couldn't help but feel like something was off. As I lay back, trying to calm my racing thoughts, something hit the side of my van with tremendous force. It was no pebble or acorn; it was a stone. The metal rang out momentarily, but I barely had time to react before something else hit the skylight and the van's roof. The sound was indescribable - a strange, muted noise, as if something was dragging across the roof and lifting away. My heart pounding in my chest, I strained my ears, listening for any sound from outside. My mind raced as I tried to rationalise what was happening. In my mind's eye, I saw a hand on the roof of the van, hitting it and scraping along before being lifted away. Was it an animal? Or was it something more sinister? Suddenly, a branch broke in the distance, and the crickets began chirping again.

An owl hooted in the darkness. I was terrified, but I couldn't leave. My curiosity got the better of me, and I needed to know what was happening. I slowly opened the skylight and peered through a one-inch gap, but all I could see was darkness. The only light source was the glow of my heater controller in the front and the USB socket in the bed. There was no moon and absolutely no light source outside. For a moment, I wondered if I was the only one out there, surrounded by an unknown and unseen danger. As I lay in my van, I couldn't help but think about the vast, silhouetted figure that had walked past the window of my van in Glen Etive, Scotland, just a few months prior. I was miles away from anyone, yet something had been there with me, watching and waiting. As I tried to settle in for the night, I couldn't shake the feeling that there was more to this forest than I could ever imagine. The final straw for me was the rhythmic sound of tapping on the side of the van. It was deliberate. It was conscious. And despite my strength in the face of danger over the years, I was scared. I sat frozen before building the courage to get into the driver's seat and turn on the lights. It took every bit of will to turn on those lights that hit the trees, and I started the engine, tearing out of the car park wearing boxer shorts and a T-shirt. On my way out, I noticed a wet smear across the paved road, entirely out of place on a hot, dry night. I didn't stop until I reached a lit parking area in a nearby town, and I never got my sunrise photo.

The call of the wild is a powerful force that draws many people into the wilderness, seeking adventure and connection with nature. Yet, the wild is also full of unknown things we don't understand. The vastness of the wilderness can be both exhilarating and terrifying as we are reminded of our own smallness and vulnerability in the face of the unknown.

While the wild may hold many mysteries, it also offers a sense of clarity and simplicity that is all too rare in our modern lives. In the wilderness, we are reminded of the essential truths of our existence: that we are part of a larger whole and are all connected in ways we cannot fully understand. As we wander through the forests and mountains, we are forced to confront our own mortality and the impermanence of all things and to find meaning and purpose in the face of this great mystery.

Ultimately, the call of the wild is to embrace the unknown, venture into the wilderness with an open heart and a sense of curiosity, and let go of our fears and preconceptions to experience the world in all its wonder and beauty. Whether we are hiking through a remote wilderness area, paddling down a wild river, or simply sitting quietly in nature, we are reminded of the deep and abiding mystery that lies at the heart of all things and of the infinite possibilities that await us when we are brave enough to answer the call of the wild.

☐

CHAPTER 10
FJAKA

A Relaxed, Carefree And Contented Peace Of Mind

"Fjaka" is a Croatian word that refers to a state of mind characterised by complete relaxation, contentment, and peace. It's a state of being where you are entirely at ease, and you feel no desire to do anything other than simply exist in the moment. In essence, fjaka is a state of mind free from stress, worry, and anxiety, and it's often associated with the Mediterranean way of life.

The concept of fjaka is deeply ingrained in Croatia's culture and way of life, especially in the country's coastal regions. It's often described as a kind of "lazy contentment," where people take the time to slow down and enjoy life's simple pleasures. This might include sitting on a beach, enjoying a leisurely meal with friends and family, or simply napping in the shade on a hot summer's day. Fjaka is not just a state of mind but also a way of life. It's about living in the moment and appreciating the simple things in life. Many Croatians believe that fjaka is essential for good mental and physical health and that taking the time to slow down and relax is an integral part of a balanced lifestyle.

Fjaka is a word that can be difficult to define, but it's often described as a state of mind that's characterised by a deep sense of relaxation, contentment, and bliss. It's a feeling of total peace and relaxation that can be experienced in a beautiful natural setting or simply enjoying life's simple pleasures.

For me, fjaka was a feeling I experienced on a journey across Europe in Kofifernweh, my converted Mercedes Sprinter van. After spending several months in the Schengen Zone, I was ready to leave the time constraints behind and explore new destinations I had always wanted to visit. Croatia was at the top of my list, with its stunning coastline, national parks, and abundant natural beauty. This part of my journey came as I reached the end of the time I was allowed to be in the Schengen Area. I'd driven from Arctic Norway, down through Finnish Lapland and to the south of Sweden, across the Øresund Strait and into Copenhagen, Denmark, where I boarded a flight to Iceland for a quick adventure dubbed Operation Fire And Ice. We'll come back to that story. On my return to Copenhagen, I had another monumental drive through Germany, Austria, Slovenia and Croatia to exit the then-Schengen borders.

The journey to Croatia was long and winding, but it was well worth it. I drove through stunning mountain ranges, across vast plains and rolling hills, and through picturesque villages and towns. Along the way, I encountered friendly locals who welcomed me with open arms, sharing stories of their own travels and experiences. Traversing the Austrian Alps was an incredible leg of this journey. It's an experience that is truly phenomenal. The majestic mountains, lush greenery, and stunning landscapes make for a carefree journey that left me feeling refreshed and rejuvenated. As I wound through the narrow roads, I was treated to panoramic views of snow-capped peaks and crystal-clear lakes. At the same time, the fresh mountain air filled my lungs and invigorated my senses. This may be an introduction to fjaka. The journey covered almost 1,500km, which naturally gave me a lot of time with my thoughts.

Throughout the journey, I found that everything I was trying to mentally resolve became more accessible with time. I found that my mind would answer most questions when I learned to relax and wait for the answers. Stressing over solutions that aren't forthcoming is incredibly unproductive. An old English proverb springs to mind, which describes this situation perfectly. It goes, "Worrying is like a rocking chair. It gives you something to do but doesn't get you anywhere." Silence can be the most productive thing, but it can be deafening. It's vital that you rule your own mind and don't allow it to rule you. This kind of revelation can only come from countless hours alone in my own mind, just like on this mammoth drive. Ultimately, remember that the only permanent thing in your life is your relationship with yourself. Everything else is temporary. Build that connection with yourself and be true to yourself. Of all the people on the planet, you will talk to yourself more than anyone. Make sure you are saying the right things. The Alps, though. With its stunning scenery and carefree atmosphere, a drive through the Austrian Alps is an unforgettable experience you will treasure for a lifetime.

One of the highlights of Croatia was visiting the Kuterevo Bear Sanctuary, a refuge for orphaned and abused brown bears located in the snow-capped mountains of central Croatia. The sanctuary is home to more than 30 bears, all of whom have been rescued from a life of suffering and abuse. The experience of seeing these magnificent creatures up close was both humbling and awe-inspiring, and it left a lasting impression on me. The care given to these bears by the team is awe-inspiring. It's genuine compassion, looking beyond their own pain to see the pain of these bears and provide a life for them. They feel the bear's pain and are moved to relieve it. There's a great quote that fits right here, and it's this: - If you see someone without a smile, give them one of yours.

As I continued my journey, I found myself drawn to the coast, with its stunning beaches and crystal-clear waters. I spent my days exploring hidden coves and bays, swimming in the sea, and soaking up the sun. One of my favourite spots was an abandoned military airfield, Zračna luka Zadar-Zaton, which had been transformed into a playground for adventurers and thrill-seekers. It was a surreal experience to wander through the destroyed, empty hangars and abandoned munitions dumps, imagining the stories of those who had once called this place home.

I found myself here alone. Solitude has an extraordinary beauty to it. This place was once so very active. It was alive with the sounds of roaring jet engines and the marching of troops not all that long ago, but now, it essentially scarred the landscape. Throughout my travels in Croatia, I found myself continually drawn back to the concept of fjaka. It was a feeling that permeated everything I did, from the simple pleasures of watching the sunset over the Adriatic to the more adventurous experiences like swimming with dolphins in the open sea or hiking through the lush forests of the national parks.

The Dalmatian coast is undoubtedly one of the most beautiful coastlines in the world, stretching from the city of Zadar in the north to Dubrovnik in the south. The coastline is dotted with numerous islands, bays, and coves, each with its own unique charm and character. As I drove south along the coast in Kofifernweh, I stopped at every opportunity to explore these hidden gems.

One of the most beautiful spots was the Pakleni Islands, just off Hvar's coast. The islands are known for their crystal clear waters and beautiful beaches. One of my favourite spots was tucked away further along the coast. A gorgeous bay surrounded by pine forests. The bay was a popular spot for yachts to anchor. I spent many hours swimming in the clear waters between editing photos and videos.

Throughout my travels along the Dalmatian coast, I was struck by the beauty and diversity of the landscape. Croatia is a country of contrasts and surprises, from the interior's snow-capped mountains to the Adriatic Sea's sun-drenched shores. And yet, despite its many wonders, there was always a sense of tranquillity and calm, a feeling of fjaka that I had rarely experienced elsewhere.

Plitvice Jezera National Park, located in central Croatia, is a stunning landscape of cascading waterfalls, turquoise lakes, and lush forests. The park is a UNESCO World Heritage site, and it is easy to see why. The park's geological makeup is unique, consisting of limestone and dolomite rock formations that have been shaped by centuries of flowing water. The park's 16 interconnected lakes, which range in colour from blue to green, are connected by a series of waterfalls that make for a truly awe-inspiring sight. One of the most impressive sights at Plitvice Jezera is the Great Waterfall, the highest waterfall in Croatia, measuring over 78 metres. Visitors can take a leisurely walk along the wooden footpaths and bridges that weave their way through the park, allowing them to get up close and personal with the waterfalls and lakes. The well-maintained paths offer stunning views of the natural beauty surrounding them.

The park's flora and fauna are equally as impressive. The dense forests are home to a variety of wildlife, including deer, boar, and wolves. The lakes teem with fish and other aquatic life, and visitors may even glimpse the elusive otter or beaver. The park has plant life, including orchids, primroses, and irises.

Ultimately, the journey through Croatia and beyond was an incredible adventure that left me with memories that will last a lifetime. And through it all, the concept of fjaka was a constant reminder to slow down, relax, and enjoy life's simple pleasures.

CHAPTER 11
FLÂNEUR

Strolling Aimlessly But Thoughtfully, Observing Your Surroundings And Contemplating The Beauty Of Everyday Life

The Mont St Michel rose from the horizon, a grand and imposing sight. I had always wanted to explore the narrow streets of this medieval town, and now I was finally getting my chance. It was early morning, and the tide was out, revealing a vast expanse of sand stretching away from the island fortress. The sun was just starting to peek over the horizon, casting a golden light across the town's walls and towers.

I wandered through the cobbled streets, taking in the intricate carvings on the buildings and the grandeur of the Abbey perched at the top of the hill. It was a place full of history and wonder, and I couldn't help but feel a sense of awe as I explored its every nook and cranny.

After a few hours, I left the Mont St Michel behind and headed south towards the lavender fields. It was a long drive, but the changing landscape made it worthwhile. I watched as the green hills and forests gave way to sun-kissed fields of golden wheat and then to rolling hills of purple lavender. The scent of the flowers filled the air, and the sight was truly captivating.

I spent a few days exploring the lavender fields of Provence, driving through winding roads that snaked through the hills and stopping at quaint little towns along the way. The sun was hot and relentless, but the beauty of the landscape made it all bearable. I'd experienced a low of -38°C in the van in Finland, and now I was experiencing a high of 46°C. I am built like a polar bear, so the heat did not favour me, but I lived in the moment. I watched as farmers harvested the lavender, their movements slow and deliberate, like a dance.

As I walked through the fields, I was struck by the sheer beauty of the lavender flowers. The vast expanse of purple stretching out before me was spine-tingling, and the sweet scent of lavender filled the air. The sound of buzzing bees and chirping crickets added to the serene atmosphere, creating an almost ethereal experience.

As the sun began to set, the colours of the lavender fields seemed to intensify, taking on a deep purple hue. The golden light of the setting sun illuminated the landscape, casting long shadows and creating a magical atmosphere. It was a moment of pure beauty as the sky became painted in shades of orange and pink. Armed with my camera, I stood in the middle of one of the fields where the lavender faded away, reaching a point on the horizon where a lone tree stood. That photo ended up on the cover of a Nikon magazine, inside which I had a twelve-page feature, which is a perfect example of the serendipity I discussed in a previous chapter. At that moment, I was wandering aimlessly and savouring the moment. Still, the opportunity arose serendipitously after the fact, and my image was front and centre on magazine stands worldwide.

I spent several days exploring the lavender fields, examining their natural beauty and learning about their history and uses. I discovered that lavender has been used for centuries for medicinal purposes and is also commonly used in perfumes, soaps, and other beauty products. As I drove away from the lavender fields, I felt a sense of peace and contentment. The beauty of the lavender touched my soul, and I was grateful for the experience. The journey continued.

The Gorges du Verdon is a natural wonder and a must-visit destination for nature enthusiasts. It is located in the south of France and is often called the Grand Canyon of Europe. The gorge is a magnificent display of nature's beauty, with its emerald-green waters and towering limestone cliffs. The river Verdon cuts through the gorge, carving out a deep canyon over 20 kilometres long and up to 700 metres deep in some places.

The Gorges du Verdon is a popular outdoor spot for hiking, climbing, kayaking, and canyoning. The hiking trails offer stunning views of the gorge and the surrounding countryside while kayaking or canoeing on the river Verdon is an unforgettable experience. The river's clear waters allow you to see the rocks and fish beneath the surface, and the towering cliffs create a dramatic backdrop.

One of the most scenic routes in the area is the Route des Crêtes, which runs along the top of the gorge. The road is narrow and winding, and the views are spectacular. From the top, you can see the entire length of the gorge and the surrounding landscape, including the nearby lavender fields.

Continuing my journey along the coast, having taken the opportunity to drive Kofifernweh through Monte Carlo, I reached the charming town of Menton. I didn't really have a set target for this drive. I just pointed forward, trusted the process, and soaked it all in. Located on the French-Italian border, this picturesque town is known for its stunning beaches and colourful buildings. I wandered through the old town's narrow streets, taking in this vibrant place's sights and sounds.

Despite the opulence and extravagance of the Riviera, I found myself drawn to the simple pleasures of the region. Walking along the beach at sunset, savouring a fresh seafood dinner at a local restaurant, or simply admiring the Mediterranean Sea's stunning views—these moments brought me the most joy. As I walked along the coastline, I couldn't help but think of the many travellers who had come before me, drawn to the beauty and allure of the Riviera. There was something special about this place, something that inspired creativity and romance. No wonder artists like Picasso and Matisse had made this their home.

My journey through the south of France reminded me of the importance of slowing down and savouring the beauty of the world around us. I had embraced the art of aimless wandering, allowing myself to be fully present in each moment and open to the beauty and wonder of the world. It was a lesson I carried with me as I continued my journey, always open to the next adventure and experience that awaited me.

From Menton, I crossed the border into Italy, and the scenery changed once again. The coastline was rugged and wild, with cliffs dropping steeply into the sea below. The towns were colourful and charming, with narrow streets that wound their way up steep hillsides. I wandered through the streets, sampling gelato and taking in the sights and sounds of this magical place.

As I travelled through France and Italy, I couldn't help but feel like a flâneur, a term coined by French poet Charles Baudelaire to describe a person who wanders aimlessly through the streets, taking in the sights and sounds of the city. I was a traveller, a wanderer, a person in love with the world and all its wonders.

In the end, my journey through France and Italy was a reminder of the beauty and diversity of this world. Every place had its unique charm and character, from the grandeur of the Mont St Michel to the tranquil lavender fields of Provence, from Menton's sandy beaches to Italy's rugged coastline. And as I travelled, I realised there was no greater joy than simply wandering, taking in the world's beauty and letting it fill me with wonder and awe. My journey continued from here into Pisa, Chamonix, and Zurich, peppered with purpose but largely with vague intent as I enjoyed the path itself.

CHAPTER 12
MUOHTA

A Sápmi Word For Snow

As I made my way through the Swedish wilderness, I was struck by the beauty of the landscape. The landscape was stark and barren but also incredibly peaceful. It was as if it had swallowed up all the world's noise and chaos, leaving only a serene silence behind.

I journeyed deeper into Lapland and was delighted to see the native wildlife. I caught glimpses of reindeer grazing on the tundra and spotted a few foxes and a wolverine darting about. The animals adapted to the harsh winter climate. Their thick fur coats and sturdy hooves made them seem almost invincible.

I was in Abisko National Park – about as far north as you can get in Sweden. As I stood outside here in Swedish Lapland, I felt a chill in the air. The leaves on the trees had already turned yellow and red, signalling the end of autumn. Winter was just around the corner, and I was excited. If I were lucky, I'd witness the first snowfall of the season. I had been eagerly waiting for this moment, timing my trip specifically for it, checking the weather forecast every day in anticipation. Finally, the day had arrived. I looked up at the sky, which was overcast and grey. Snowflakes began to fall from the sky, drifting gently down to the ground.

The first few snowflakes were small and delicate, but they soon began to multiply, forming a beautiful white blanket that covered everything in sight. The sound of the snow falling was almost like a silent lullaby, peaceful and calming. Walking through the snow-covered landscape, I felt a sense of wonder and awe. Everything was so still and quiet, and the snow seemed to muffle all the sounds around me. It was as if the world had slowed down and was taking a deep breath. I watched as the snowflakes continued to fall, swirling around me like tiny dancers. Each flake was unique, and I marvelled at their intricate designs. The landscape was transformed, and everything looked so pure and pristine under the blanket of snow.

I spotted a group of reindeer, their antlers covered in snow, as they made their way through the tundra. Seeing the majestic creatures against the snowy landscape was a picture-perfect moment.

As the snow continued falling, I knew that winter had arrived. It was a moment I would never forget, a magical experience I was grateful to have witnessed. In Lapland, the arrival of winter is not just a change in the weather; it is a celebration of life. The locals embrace the snow, and all that comes with it, from the activities like skiing and snowshoeing to the warm and comforting food perfect for cold winter nights. For me, the first snowfall in Lapland reminded me of nature's beauty and the wonders it can bring. It was a moment of pure magic. I knew it was just the beginning of an unforgettable winter adventure in Lapland.

Along the way, I also got to experience the unique culture of Lapland. I visited a traditional Sámi village and learned about their way of life. I was fascinated by their traditional clothing, designed to keep them warm in freezing temperatures, and their reindeer husbandry practices.

On this journey through Swedish Lapland and into Finish Lapland, I realised that Lapland was more than just a beautiful landscape and a place to visit. It was a place that had a soul, a spirit, and a story. It was a place that had captured my heart. Lapland is the name for an area inhabited by the native Sámi people. The Sápmi nation is a cultural and geographic region. It encompasses parts of northern Scandinavia and the Kola Peninsula in Russia, spanning Norway, Sweden, Finland, and Russia. The Sámi are indigenous people with a rich cultural heritage. They are characterised by their close relationship with the Arctic environment and reindeer herding traditions. The Sápmi nation represents the Sámi's shared history, language, customs, and efforts to preserve their unique identity in the face of social, economic, and environmental challenges.

I returned to Lapland many times, but once, my objective was to find Santa's cabin. It goes without saying that this was high on my list of objectives in Lapland. The cabin sits atop a fell in Finnish Lapland near the town of Levi. I've been fortunate enough to ski to the cabin a few times and the story behind it is captivating. It's the story of a little boy named Nikolas.

His father was a poor hunter who struggled to provide for him. Nikolas' life was turned upside down when his mother died, leaving him alone with his father. Nikolas was forced to grow up quickly, learning how to fend for himself in the harsh Finnish wilderness.

One winter, as Nikolas was out hunting in the woods, he came across a group of friendly elves who were lost and in need of help. Nikolas befriended the elves and offered to guide them back to their home, hidden deep in the forest. As a reward for his kindness, the elves offered to grant Nikolas a wish. Nikolas asked for nothing more than a gift for his father, who he knew was struggling to provide for him. The elves promised to return the following winter and fulfil his wish.

Over the course of the following year, Nikolas waited patiently for the return of the elves. As Christmas approached, he began to lose hope that they would ever return. But on Christmas Eve, the elves appeared, bearing gifts for Nikolas and his father. Nikolas's gift was a miniature wooden toy horse carved by the elves. Overjoyed, Nikolas showed the toy horse to his father, who was touched by his son's gift.

Moved by the generosity and kindness of the elves, Nikolas decided to repay their kindness by becoming their caretaker. He set out into the woods with his trusty reindeer, helping the elves with their tasks and keeping them safe from harm.

Over time, Nikolas became a beloved community figure known for his kindness and generosity. The villagers began to leave gifts for him under the Christmas tree, and Nikolas became known as the giver of gifts. As Nikolas grew older, he took on the role of Joulupukki, or Santa Claus, bringing joy and happiness to children all over the world. Every Christmas, as he travels the globe on his sleigh, he remembers the kindness of the elves who changed his life forever.

The snow is often associated with the festive season and for good reason. There is something magical about how the snow transforms the landscape, turning it into a winter wonderland. The snowflakes falling from the sky are delicate and intricate, each unique in its design. The white blanket of snow that covers everything in sight creates a sense of purity and tranquillity that is perfect for the holiday season.

The snow also has a way of bringing out the generosity in people. As the weather turns colder, people begin to think of those who are less fortunate, and many organisations and charities start fundraising campaigns to help those in need. The snow inspires us to think beyond ourselves and to focus on the needs of others. It reminds us that Christmas is a time for giving and that by sharing our resources and love, we can make a difference in those around us. As you enjoy the beauty of the snow, remember the joy of generosity and the difference it can indirectly make in the world. Snowflakes are one of the most fragile things in nature, but just look at their power when they stick together.

The harshness of snow and winter can be unforgiving, transforming the world into a frozen landscape that challenges even the hardiest souls. In the remote corners of

Norway, where the biting wind whips across the icy fjords, fishermen face the daunting task of navigating treacherous waters and enduring bone-chilling temperatures. Yet, these resilient souls have honed their craft and developed simple yet effective methods to confront the winter's wrath.

With years of experience and ancestral wisdom passed down through generations, Norwegian fishermen have learned to adapt and thrive in the harshest conditions. Their vessels, sturdy and built to withstand the relentless onslaught of winter, become their sanctuary amidst the frozen expanse. With each passing storm, they navigate the icy waters, their movements a dance of resilience and skill.

These intrepid seafarers have mastered the art of reading nature's signs, recognising subtle shifts in wind patterns and cloud formations that hint at imminent danger. They know when to retreat to the safety of sheltered coves and harbour, finding solace in the warmth of their hearths as they patiently wait for the storm to pass.

They rely on age-old techniques in freezing temperatures to keep warm and preserve their catch. They don layer upon layer of thick wool and waterproof garments, protecting themselves from the bitter cold that gnaws at their bones. Their hands, calloused and weathered, deftly handle the nets and lines, hardened by years of exposure to the elements.

In these simple yet effective ways, Norwegian fishermen navigate the unforgiving winter with stoic determination. They embrace the challenges the snow and ice present, seeing them not as insurmountable obstacles but as an intrinsic part of their way of life. Their resilience and resourcefulness testify to the strength of the human spirit, reminding us that simple methods can yield extraordinary results even in the face of adversity.

As we witness these brave fishermen's trials, we are reminded of the power of human ingenuity and the remarkable ability to adapt to our surroundings. Their story inspires us, urging us to meet the harshness of winter and its challenges with courage and simplicity. In their unwavering determination, we find a profound lesson – that even in the coldest times, the human spirit can ignite a flame that melts away the harshest winters.

CHAPTER 13

SKÖP

Disorder And Confusion

Totally insane! These are the words often uttered by Adobe Senior Principal Director Russell Brown. Russell commissioned me to shoot an aeroplane in flight from another plane soaring over glacial rivers in Iceland's winter landscape. As I soared through the vast expanse of Iceland's skies, the exhilarating rush of flight consumed me. Inside the humble confines of the Cessna, I felt a sense of liberation. This freedom only comes from being suspended between heaven and earth. The wind whispered in my ears as I peered out of the open window, my camera firmly in my frozen hand, ready to capture the extraordinary scene unfolding before my eyes.

Another trike plane joined us in the aerial ballet in perfect harmony, flying in formation as if in a carefully choreographed dance. With each passing moment, the world below transformed into a beautiful canvas, waiting to be immortalised through my lens. The camaraderie and shared passion reverberated through the cockpit, connecting us in a bond forged by our mutual love for the art of flight.

And then, it appeared—a moment frozen in time, etched forever in my memory. Against an azure sky, a frozen glacial river snaked through the Icelandic landscape. It glistened like a silver ribbon, shimmering in the sunlight, its icy surface adorned with delicate patterns of frost. The contrast was striking—the piercing blue of the water, the pristine white of the ice, and the vibrant colours of the Icelandic flag painted on the aircraft beneath us.

As I framed the shot, the vibrant red, white, and blue of the plane's livery stood out boldly against the ethereal backdrop. It was a testament to the spirit of Iceland, a nation proud of its heritage and natural wonders. The colours seemed to dance with an energy all their own, embodying the resilience and beauty of this untamed land. It was a snapshot of patriotism and freedom, captured from a unique perspective, high above the world below.

In that single photograph, time stood still. It encapsulated the sheer joy of flight, the exhilaration of capturing a moment that would never be repeated. It was a visual symphony, where the harmonious composition of colours, shapes, and elements fused into a masterpiece. Through that lens, I felt connected to something greater, a fleeting glimpse of the extraordinary beauty beyond our everyday lives.

I carried that photograph as I descended from the heavens, and the Cessna gently touched on Icelandic soil at Reykjavík airport. It served as a reminder of the incredible experiences that await us when we dare to take flight, literally and metaphorically. It spoke of the unyielding spirit of exploration. These endless possibilities unfold when we immerse ourselves in the world's wonders. And above all, it embodied the magic of photography, the ability to capture a single moment and preserve it as a treasure—a testament to the beauty surrounding us, waiting to be discovered, shared, and cherished.

The next time I set foot on the rugged land of Iceland was to meet Russell at Keflavik airport before a crazy adventure. A sense of anticipation and excitement coursed through my veins. I had embarked on a unique experience, a photographic journey across the country's mesmerising south coast. My mission with Russell was to capture the essence of contrasts, the dance between fire and ice that defined this extraordinary land. This is Operation Fire And Ice.

Accompanied by local guide Einar and a fire-breather named Ivar, we set off with another local guide named Boggi, who possessed an intimate knowledge of the region. Our first major destination was an ethereal ice cave hidden within the Vatnajökull glacier. With each step, the icy air pierced through my bones. With every breath, I marvelled at sights before me, a harmonious meeting of elements that stirred the depths of my creative spirit. The ethereal beauty of the frozen chamber unfolded before my eyes, captivating me with its glistening walls of crystalline ice. With each step, crunching snow echoed, adding to the sense of wonder that permeated the air.

With his flaming torch in hand, Ivar brought a perfect element of juxtaposition to the frozen sanctuary. As he stepped further into the cave, he unleashed his mastery, breathing life into the depths of this frozen realm. The flames erupted from his mouth, dancing and flickering with an otherworldly glow, casting vibrant orange light against the dark blue, icy backdrop. This colour balance is why we, as humans, are so attracted to sunsets. The orange sun against the blue sky is represented perfectly in the position of these two colours across from one another in the colour wheel. They're complementary colours. With this glow, it was as if the cavern came alive, a symphony of fire and ice, the meeting of two elemental forces.

As I watched in awe, giant balls of fire burst forth, illuminating the ancient ice formations with radiant warmth. The flames seemed to dance perfectly with the delicate icicles that hung from the ceiling as if engaged in a tender duet between heat and cold. It was a perfect analogy for Iceland's expansive glaciers and 30 active volcano systems. Once silent witnesses to the passing of time, the cave walls now reverberated with the crackling and hissing of the flames, creating an exhilarating yet surreal soundtrack created for the sake of art.

I was lost in the contrast—the vibrant, mesmerising flames against the sheer, delicate beauty of the ice. Every flicker and roar of the flames cast dramatic shadows that danced along the icy contours, breathing life into the frozen canvas. It was a visual spectacle that etched itself into my memory, a moment of magic and wonder that could never be replicated.

As Ivar continued his fiery display, his presence reminded me of the resilience and strength within each of us. In the face of the cold and unforgiving nature of the ice cave, his flames represented the human spirit's ability to create warmth, light, and beauty even in the harshest environments.

But beyond the sheer spectacle, there was a deeper connection, a shared experience of pushing boundaries and defying expectations. The chaos was there to be embraced.

As we emerged from the depths of the ice cave, a renewed sense of awe and inspiration accompanied us. The memories of that fiery performance against the icy backdrop will forever be imprinted in my heart. It was a testament to the power of exploration, the unyielding curiosity that drives us to uncover the world's hidden wonders. And in that frozen sanctuary, we discovered a profound truth—that in the face of the most inhospitable environments, the human spirit has the remarkable capacity to ignite hope, warmth, and beauty, even within the depths of an ice cave.

Leaving the ice cave behind, we ventured deeper into the Icelandic wilderness, seeking the enigmatic Yoda Cave. The cave, tucked away amidst the untamed beauty of the landscape, seemed to hold ancient secrets. With our cameras poised, we delved into the cavern's depths, capturing the interplay of light and shadow as it danced upon the rugged rock formations. With his fiery breath, Ivar added a supernatural element to the scene as if he were an emissary from another realm, breathing life into the tale the cave had to tell.

With our minds ablaze with creativity, we continued our journey, guided by the desire to capture the unexpected. Before the break of dawn, we made our way to Stokksnes, a vast black sand beach framed by dramatic dunes. Our eyes widened at the sight of a solitary washing machine perched upon the sand, an incongruous and whimsical sight against nature's raw beauty. We'd carried the washing machine across the black sand and up to the crest of a dune for another crazy photo. Ivar transformed from a fire-breather to a mad scientist, his flames replaced by sparks of eccentricity. We immortalised this impulsive moment, blending the surreal with the serene. As the first blue light of dawn turned to a golden glow upon the rugged landscape, the stage was being set for a remarkable photoshoot. Nestled along the southeastern coast, Stokksnes offered a surreal and ethereal backdrop for a project called 'The Interstellar Trash Machine.' It was a bold artistic statement, aiming to shed light on the vast amount of waste humanity generates, even extending to space junk.

The centrepiece of the shoot was the washing machine transformed into a symbol of our collective waste. Against the stark contrast of the black sand dunes, the washing machine stood like an alien artefact, a testament to our responsibility to protect and preserve our planet. Outfitted with a bike wheel and adorned with flashing lights, it stood as a striking representation of our consumption-driven culture.

Stokksnes was a place of otherworldly beauty. The black sand stretched like an endless sea, its volcanic origins adding an element of mystery to the landscape. The towering presence of Vestrahorn, a majestic mountain range, provided a dramatic backdrop. Its jagged peaks seemed to pierce the heavens, inviting a sense of awe and reverence.

As the shoot unfolded, the changing light danced upon the scene, transforming the atmosphere with each passing moment. The soft hues of pre-dawn slowly gave way to a kaleidoscope of colours as the sun breached the horizon. Once shrouded in darkness, the black sand revealed intricate patterns and textures. At the same time, the washing machine, with its flickering lights, took on an almost mystical quality.

With the rising sun, the light bathed the surroundings in a warm embrace, breathing life into the landscape. The golden light painted the dunes and mountain peaks, casting an enchanting glow and illuminating the project's meaning. The interplay of light and shadow added depth and dimension, evoking a sense of introspection and contemplation.

As the shoot progressed, the interstellar trash machine became a captivating focal point against the ever-changing canvas of Stokksnes. Its symbolism grew more vital as a stark reminder of our role in safeguarding the planet and tackling the mounting waste issue. The juxtaposition of the man-made washing machine against nature's raw, untamed beauty was a visual metaphor that resonated deeply.

At that moment, a powerful statement emerged amidst the shifting light and the windswept dunes. 'The Interstellar Trash Machine' was more than just a photo shoot; it was a call to action. It invited viewers to reflect upon our actions' impact on Earth and beyond. And as the sun continued its ascent, painting the world with its vibrant palette, it reminded us of the beauty of preserving our planet and our responsibility to be stewards of our existence.

Iceland revealed itself as a muse throughout our adventure, inspiring us with its untamed spirit and awe-inspiring landscapes. The juxtaposition of fire and ice was not merely a photographic project; it embodied the essence of Iceland itself, a land shaped by the ever-shifting dance between opposing forces. Each click of the shutter captured a fragment of this elemental symphony, a testament to the limitless possibilities of artistic expression.

As our journey drew to a close, we carried the memories of our Icelandic odyssey deep within our souls. The fire and ice, the ethereal ice caves, the enigmatic Yoda Cave, and the whimsy of a washing machine on black sand dunes—all became chapters in the story we had woven through our photographs. Iceland had gifted us with more than just extraordinary images; it had ignited a spark within us, a creative fire that would continue to burn long after we depart from this magical land of fire and ice, and it all stemmed from a totally insane idea.

Life gives us a choice: to embark on a daring adventure or accept a mundane existence. In moments when we discard caution and surrender ourselves to the winds of uncertainty, our dreams find wings to soar to extraordinary realms. Regrets often stem from opportunities untaken, reminding us that the essence of wisdom lies in embracing risks. We unlock the door to authentic growth and profound self-discovery by leaping into the unknown. Playing it safe becomes an inadequate strategy in life, as we are urged to embrace the ambiguous, seize chances, and forge ahead unencumbered by remorse. The grandest rewards are invariably reserved for those who dare to tread the path of audacity. Hence, we are urged to cultivate the courage to live the life our imaginations have long envisaged. Just as the vast ocean reveals its splendour when we relinquish the safety of the shore, true beauty unfolds when we embrace uncertainty and venture fearlessly into the waves of possibility. If not now, when?

CHAPTER 14
NO WORRIES

A Laid-Back Attitude Emphasising Calmness

When I was working as a wedding photographer in partnership with my best friend Peter, we worked hard to promote our business. We found ourselves shooting weddings internationally; we were in Australia on this occasion. At this time, I found myself in the final round of judging for the Wildlife Photographer Of The Year competition, too. I was still finding my place as a photographer, hence the breadth between the two subjects, but this was an exciting time. Peter and I had planned a trip to The Pinnacles to take photos of the Milky Way above the iconic rock formations – astrophotography. We set out from Perth in the late afternoon, eager to capture the golden hour light and the stunning sunset. However, as we drove further north, we realised how vast Australia is. The road seemed to stretch forever, and we soon realised we wouldn't make it to The Pinnacles before nightfall. In fact, as the road continued, we decided to cut our losses as we would be out for far too long.

The night sky was completely clear, with no moonlight to distort our view of the Milky Way. Disappointed, we decided to pull over and make the most of the situation. We found a spot off the beaten track and set up our equipment. We began taking photos, entirely captivated by the stunning display of stars above us.

While focused on capturing the perfect shot, we suddenly heard a thumping sound nearby. We froze, unsure of what could be making the noise. It was pitch black, and we couldn't see anything beyond the reach of our camera's flash, which was our only source of light. We had a fraction of a second of pure brightness to try and see what was making the sounds, blinded momentarily after firing the strobe, which served only as a light, not a tool for photography.

The noise grew louder, and we could hear something bouncing towards us. We saw absolutely nothing, but from the sound alone, this thing was big. Our hearts racing, we were sure we were about to be attacked by some wild animal. Being from out of town, as it were, it took a while to realise that we were being snuck up by what sounded like the world's most enormous kangaroo.

We very quietly devised a plan to get back to the car, parked around a corner, about a minute or two away. As we moved, the bouncing moved. It was following us, but we had to remain calm. There was no choice in the situation than to stay level-headed, and We both breathed a sigh of relief, grateful that we weren't in any real danger. We continued taking photos, now with an added sense of adrenaline-fueled excitement. That night, we may not have made it to The Pinnacles, but thanks to remaining calm, we had an unforgettable experience.

As a travel photographer constantly immersed in new situations and places, I've realised the profound significance of embracing the concept of "no worries" in alleviating the undue stresses of everyday life. While capturing fleeting moments and seeking out extraordinary scenes, I've learned that worrying only hinders our ability to fully embrace the present and appreciate the beauty surrounding us.

In my nomadic existence, I've encountered countless situations that could have easily caused anxiety to creep into my thoughts. From navigating unfamiliar streets with a language barrier to facing unpredictable weather conditions during a shoot, there have been numerous instances where worry could have taken hold. Yet, I've discovered that worrying achieves nothing but robbing us of the precious moments that make life truly remarkable. Each moment is a canvas waiting to be painted with light and emotion. It requires a focused mind, a calm spirit, and the ability to adapt to ever-changing circumstances. There is no room for worry when chasing the perfect shot because worry only clouds our perception and prevents us from fully immersing ourselves in the magic of the present.

I've found that adopting a "no worries" mindset allows me to approach every new situation with a sense of curiosity and openness. Instead of dwelling on what could go wrong, I embrace the unknown and trust in my ability to navigate any challenges that may arise. Perhaps it came from growing up just at the right time to hear Timon and Pumbaa sing all about the Swahili phrase, "Hakuna Matata." It's a liberating feeling, knowing that I have the power to control my reactions and choose a perspective rooted in positivity and resilience.

Through my lens, I've witnessed awe-inspiring landscapes, encountered fascinating cultures, and connected with remarkable individuals. In these moments, worries dissolve into the background, replaced by a deep sense of wonder and appreciation for the world around me. I've come to understand that worry, in its essence, is a product of the mind projecting into an uncertain future. At the same time, the true beauty lies in the present, where worries hold no sway.

When we embrace the "no worries" philosophy, we grant ourselves permission to let go of the weight that anchors us down. We allow ourselves to be fully present, to engage with the world in all its vivid hues and intricacies. We become attuned to the subtle nuances of life—the gentle whispers of the wind, the mesmerising dance of sunlight, and the infectious laughter of strangers.

The "no worries" concept is not an invitation to be careless or negligent. It is a call to release the unnecessary burden of worries that can obscure our ability to live fully and authentically. It reminds us to be proactive and prepared, to find solutions rather than dwelling on problems. It encourages us to cultivate resilience and trust in our own capabilities.

In my journey as a travel photographer, beyond merely one occasion in Australia with a sneaky kangaroo stalking me in the bush, I've come to appreciate that life is an ever-unfolding tapestry of moments—some filled with joy and others with challenges. By embracing the philosophy of "no worries," we can approach each moment with grace, allowing ourselves to be fully present, find beauty in unexpected places, and navigate the intricacies of life with a lighter heart and a clearer mind.

As I continue to venture into new landscapes, documenting the world's wonders through my lens, I carry with me the profound wisdom of "no worries." It serves as a guiding light, reminding me to let go of unnecessary stress, embrace the unknown with open arms, and find solace in knowing that life's journey is meant to be experienced, one worry-free step at a time. Going a step beyond, this principle also applies to our attitude when we go about our everyday life and allow our mood to be affected by others. In the vast tapestry of life, it is crucial to remember that we hold the power to protect our peace, spirit, and joy. We must not allow the behaviour and actions of others to permeate our being and dictate our emotional state. We are the guardians of our own happiness, and by choosing not to be swayed by negativity, we preserve the purity of our own essence. Instead, let us rise above the turbulence, embracing the serenity that comes from within, and radiate a steadfast light that remains untarnished by external circumstances. Our spirit is resilient, our heart is boundless, and our joy is unwavering when we choose not to grant permission for others to disrupt our inner harmony.

CHAPTER 15
NÍŁCH'I

Inner Strength

The Navajo people, the Diné, embody the resilient spirit that dances with the winds and whispers through the canyons of their sacred land. They are the weavers of dreams, painting their stories on the tapestry of time with vibrant threads of tradition and wisdom. Their rich and vibrant culture is like a sacred fire that burns brightly in their hearts, illuminating the path for generations to come. From their ancient roots to the present day, the Navajo have navigated the labyrinth of challenges with grace and unwavering determination. With every step they take, they honour the legacy of their ancestors, forging a future that blends the ancient with the modern, embracing the strength of their heritage and the beauty of their aspirations.

At the heart of Navajo culture lies a profound connection to the natural world, an unbreakable bond woven by the threads of kinship and respect. The Navajo find solace in the vastness of the desert and draw inspiration from the resilience of the towering mesas. They hear the mountains' whispers and speak the stars' language. With each sunrise, they greet the day with gratitude, embracing the opportunity to walk in harmony with the Earth and all its creatures. They understand that their destinies are intertwined with the sacred web of life. In their footsteps, they leave imprints of love, stewardship, and reverence for the land that nourishes their spirits.

In the Navajo people, one finds a tapestry of stories, songs, and traditions that span countless generations. They are the storytellers, passing down ancient wisdom and sacred knowledge, preserving the essence of their identity with every word spoken. The Navajo cherish the power of community, for they know they are strong together. Their greatest strength lies in unity. They celebrate the diversity within their tribe, weaving together the threads of different talents and perspectives to create a vibrant and harmonious whole. With their warm smiles and open hearts, the Navajo extend a hand of friendship and welcome all who seek to understand the beauty and resilience that lies within their culture.

With their indomitable spirit, a deep reverence for nature, and rich cultural heritage, the Navajo inspire us to embrace our roots, honour our connection with the world around us, and weave a tapestry of unity, love, and resilience in our own lives. I was lucky enough to learn this first-hand. I explored the Navajo Nation, met local people, and heard their stories. Their inner strength is evident, mainly when considering all they've been through as a people, but whilst in their lands, I had to find my inner strength.

After a Photoshop World Conference in Las Vegas, during which I presented a class on travel photography to a packed room at The Mirage, I took the opportunity to unwind and explore. Firstly, with my friend Mark Heaps, we headed out on a Route 66 adventure on Triumph Tiger motorbikes. As we embarked on our journey along Route 66, the iconic Mother Road, I felt a sense of adventure tingling in my veins. The sun-kissed landscapes of Arizona, Nevada, and Utah stretched out before me, promising a ride filled with captivating vistas and hidden treasures. Leaving behind the dazzling lights of Las Vegas, I immersed myself in a tapestry of rugged desert terrain. The echoes of the past whispered through the rustling tumbleweeds, interspersed with signs of modern America.

The asphalt ribbon of Route 66 guided us through a timeless journey, revealing the remnants of a bygone era. As I rode through the arid expanses of Arizona, the ghost towns whispered stories of pioneers, cowboys, and dreams lost and found. The weathered facades of old motels and diners stood as testaments to the glory days of a once bustling highway. Each mile revealed a new chapter in the history of the American West, and I marvelled at the resilience and spirit of those who had travelled this path before me.

Venturing off the beaten path, we navigated the dirt roads crisscrossing the Arizona and Nevada landscapes. The wheels of my motorcycle stirred up clouds of red dust as I delved deeper into the untamed wilderness. Towering saguaros and Joshua trees stood sentinel, their gnarled branches reaching for the boundless sky. The solitude of these remote stretches was humbling and invigorating as I became one with the untamed spirit of the desert.

Returning to Las Vegas, I carried the memories of the open road and the beauty I had witnessed along the way. The journey had awakened a deep appreciation for the vastness of the American Southwest, its rugged charm, and the stories etched into its very soul. As I stood amidst the hustle and bustle of slot city once more, I knew that my ride along Route 66 and the dusty dirt roads had forever imprinted upon me a sense of freedom, wonder, and a profound connection to the timeless landscapes that define this captivating region. The fuel it had given to my spirit was immense. It prepared me for a near immediate departure on the second adventure – a road trip in an SUV with Sian Elizabeth where we aimed to drive a giant loop to Monument Valley, taking in Zion, Bryce, White Pocket, and as much as we could along the way.

There's a part of me that yearns to understand. Mainly in my sights is the natural world. I have an insatiable desire to understand everything around me, both near and far, which is something to bear in mind for this next story or two.

While in the area of Hurricane, Utah, we searched for a short hike. We learned that Red Cliffs National Conservation Area was close-by, so we headed that way for late afternoon.

As we embarked on our hiking adventure, I felt a surge of anticipation for the hidden wonders that lay ahead. Following the path of a dry river, I was drawn deeper into the heart of this ancient desert sanctuary. The sun painted the red cliffs in fiery orange and deep crimson hues, casting a mesmerising glow over the rugged landscape.

The rhythmic crunch of my footsteps echoed through the canyon as I traced the path of the dry watercourse, its existence hinted at by the scattered rocks and remnants of past torrents. The trail led me past weathered caves that seemed to guard secrets of a forgotten time. Their rocky entrances beckoned me to explore their depths. Still, aside from a few photos inside one particularly inviting, wide cave, I pressed on, eager to witness the unfolding beauty of the landscape.

As I ascended the stepped, dry waterfalls, a sense of triumph mingled with the awe that filled my heart. The towering cliffs seemed to whisper tales of resilience and timelessness while the silence enveloped me like a comforting embrace. Each level conquered brought me closer to the heart of the wilderness, revealing increasingly smaller canyons that offered a sanctuary from the outside world.

In these narrow canyons, the scale of the world transformed. I marvelled at the intricate layers of rock, each one a testament to the passage of time. Sunbeams filtered through narrow cracks, casting ephemeral patterns on the canyon walls. With each dry waterfall I approached, the climbs became increasingly more difficult. Eventually, Sian decided to wait behind while I went ahead alone. I held a rope fastened to the rocks, leading me up to the next level. Alone, I noticed that the air carried a crispness that invigorated my senses, reminding me of the remarkable power of nature to shape and mould the world around us.

I walked a short way, out of sight and sound of Sian, until the canyon forked. The sun was setting fast, and the cool air flowing in the canyon became darker. As I reached the fork, I noticed a depression in the rock. It was perfectly placed to serve as the foreground in one last photo before I turned back around. I got out my tripod and lined up my shot, making minor adjustments to get the framing just right. I noticed a slight rustle in some bushes that lined the gentle slope of the canyon where the two channels met. I didn't think much of it, and after glancing in that direction, I returned to work with my camera. I squatted down to my camera bag to get a filter for my lens, and a different sound came from the exact origin of the rustle. This time, a soft thud accompanied by what sounded like a very short, sharp exhale. The air turned silent as my full, wide-eyed attention turned to the bushes. I was in cougar territory, and this otherwise extremely stealthy cat had clearly made a mistake in creating these sounds. Rather than become dinner, it was time to eat some of my own. I grabbed everything and went back the way I came, backwards. With my attention fully fixed on the bushes, tuned to detect the slightest movement, I went as fast as possible towards where I had left Sian without running.

I reached the dry waterfall with the rope, and there she was, photographing something on the canyon wall, perhaps the texture or a flower; I don't know, and quite frankly, I didn't care. I knew we needed to leave but I didn't want to alarm her. I quickly reached her level and said, "I'm hungry; let's go now." She raised an eyebrow, clearly seeing straight through my attempt at being subtle, and said, "Right, ok." My mind still fixated on the noise of what I was sure was a mountain lion; we walked back approximately half a mile to where we left the car, following the canyon walls. Whenever she stopped for a photo or to look at an interesting plant, I hurried her along, constantly scanning over my shoulder, attentive to everything around us. She kept asking me what was up, and I was doing a terrible job of keeping the situation calm, but I pulled all the strength I had inside together and got us out of there. My mind kept telling me to check the rim of the canyon – the high ground. I could swear I saw that mountain lion looking down at us, quickly ducking and flattening its ears as I made eye contact.

As we retraced our steps back to the trailhead, I carried with me the memories of this unforgettable journey through the Red Cliffs Conservation Area and the insane level of uncertainty and fear that came over me, culminating in a huge desire to protect us both. Only afterwards, when we got to Denny's in Hurricane, the beauty and solitude of the canyons and the raw, untouched nature that surrounded me left an indelible mark on my soul. It was a reminder that in the heart of the wilderness, where the dry river meets the cliffs, one can find solace, inspiration, and a profound connection to the ancient forces that have shaped our world, even if we don't necessarily see those forces. There's a lot to see, but there's also a lot that remains unseen.

The following evening things got even stranger, even if only for a second or so. Following a day in Zion National Park, it again became time to eat, so after the sun had set, we headed back into Hurricane. We were entering town from the east. Hurricane is in Utah, near the Nevada border. The direction we were facing and the night sky ahead of us was the sky over Nevada. This is important information as I set the scene.

Driving along State Route 9 in Utah is stunning by day, but in darkness, there isn't an awful lot to look at. Both tired but satisfied with our adventure and photography achievements that day, our eyes were fixed through the windscreen, taking in the road ahead and anticipating what we might eat for dinner. In the sky ahead, high up in the distance, we suddenly saw a light appear. It appeared just like a very bright star with a slightly blue tinge, and despite being static when it appeared, it immediately shot downwards. What was extremely high up was suddenly just a fraction above the horizon. As suddenly as it appeared and started moving, it stopped and disappeared. It was as if it switched off and faded away into nothing.

This whole thing happened in about a second or so – definitely no more than two seconds. We were both looking straight at it and immediately, there was a 'Did you see that too?' moment between us. Both confirmed that we saw the same strange thing happen in the night sky straight ahead of us, and we discussed what it could have been. A shooting star? No, it went straight down, had no tail, and it wasn't a consistent speed. An aircraft? Perhaps a helicopter? Still no, it started too high, ended too low, and was incredibly fast. We both hesitantly came to the same conclusion: UFO. I realised that we were facing Nevada. As soon as we got to the restaurant, I checked my map and worked out that from where we were, a little over 100 miles ahead of us, was the Nevada Test and Training Range, more commonly known as Area 51. Did we see something from another world inside our own? It certainly seemed that way, and after an incredible adventure in the American South West, this was undoubtedly a story to tell.

Dealing with things we don't understand or can't see requires a deep reservoir of inner strength. In these moments of uncertainty and mystery, we are tested, our resilience and fortitude called upon. Different situations elicit different responses, and in any case, it takes courage to confront the unknown, acknowledge our limitations, and accept that there are forces at work beyond our comprehension. Building inner strength begins with cultivating a mindset of curiosity and openness. It involves embracing the discomfort of not having all the answers and, instead, fostering a willingness to explore, learn, and grow. Developing inner strength also entails creating a sense of trust in ourselves and the greater universe. Trusting that we have the capacity to face the challenges before us and that the answers will unfold in due time. Through self-reflection, resilience-building practices, and seeking support from people we trust, we can strengthen our inner resolve and navigate uncharted territories with greater confidence and grace.

To build inner strength, it's important to cultivate self-awareness and embrace self-compassion. This involves being honest with ourselves about our strengths and limitations, acknowledging our vulnerabilities, and treating ourselves with kindness and understanding. Practising mindfulness and meditation can help us develop a greater sense of presence and resilience, enabling us to face the unknown with a calm and centred mindset. Believe in yourself and all that you are. There is something inside each of us that's greater than any obstacle. Sometimes it may be the case that you will realise just how strong you are once strength becomes your only choice.

Our inner strength pushes us to try new things and take calculated risks, so take the strength you have and use it.

Maybe it won't work out, but maybe it will. Maybe finding out will be the most incredible adventure ever. And remember this, which we can all relate to: There are people less qualified than you doing the things you want to do simply because they decided to believe in themselves.

CHAPTER 16
BIFRÖST

The Rainbow Bridge

In Norse mythology, the Rainbow Bridge is known as Bifröst. Bifröst is a celestial bridge that connects the realm of the gods, Asgard, with the mortal realm, Midgard (Earth). It is described as a radiant and shimmering bridge, often portrayed as a rainbow or a burning bridge made of fire.

Bifröst plays a significant role in mythology as it serves as the primary means of communication and travel between the different realms. Bifröst is said to be guarded by the god Heimdall, who stands watch at its entrance. The bridge is believed to be incredibly strong, but it is said to tremble and shake under the weight of the gods and other divine beings as they traverse it.

According to Norse mythology, during the cataclysmic event of Ragnarök, it is prophesied that Bifröst will be destroyed. The bridge will shatter, collapsing under the weight of giants and dark forces, signifying the end of the current world order.

The Rainbow Bridge, or Bifröst, symbolises connection, passage, and transcendence between realms in Norse mythology, representing the link between the gods and humanity. Do you know what it sounds like to me? It sounds a lot like the northern lights. It shines and shimmers;

it isn't always present, and it 'shakes' occasionally. Indeed the Norse way of explaining the mysterious northern lights was their inclusion of bifröst in their mythology. We're at a time in history where we can explain so much of the world around us, so we know exactly what the northern lights really are. Imagine being at a different point in the human story where the sun wasn't understood, we weren't aware of the presence of an atmosphere around our planet, and we didn't have satellites and other monitoring equipment that could explain the phenomenon of the aurora. There are many stories from earlier cultures to explain the most incredible light show on Earth, but also different variants of it. The bifröst perfectly describes the arcs we get when the northern lights span from one horizon to the other. Still, sometimes we get auroras in different forms.

The dancing lights of the Northern Lights were believed to be the shimmering armour and enchanted weapons of the celestial Norse warriors. These divine warriors, led by the valiant Odin, the Allfather, would ride across the night sky, engaging in epic battles against the forces of darkness. As their swords clashed and their armour glowed with ethereal brilliance, the celestial warriors would create a captivating display of lights, enchanting mortals below and reminding them of the eternal struggle between light and darkness.

According to Inuit mythology, the Northern Lights resulted from the spirits of their ancestors gathering in the celestial realm to celebrate and dance. As the spirits twirled and weaved through the night sky, their joyful footsteps created a heart-stirring symphony of colour and movement. It was believed that witnessing this celestial dance brought good fortune and blessings. The spirits would bring messages from the spirit world to guide and protect their descendants on Earth.

The ancient Sami people believed that the Northern Lights were the magical weavings of Beaivi, the cosmic weaver and the sun goddess. Beaivi was a powerful and mystical being who wove the fabric of the universe together. As she worked diligently on her cosmic loom, her vibrant threads would intertwine and illuminate the night sky, creating an awe-inspiring display of swirling colours and patterns. It was said that the lights held hidden messages and prophecies within their intricate designs, accessible only to those who possessed a pure heart and a keen eye.

In Finnish folklore, the Northern Lights were associated with the mystical creature, the "Firefox." Firefox was known as Revontulet. These mischievous and cunning foxes were said to have tails imbued with magical powers. When they scampered across the heavens, their tails would brush against the snow-capped mountains, creating a mesmerising spectacle of fiery lights. The Revontulet used the Northern Lights as a gateway to travel between worlds, leaving behind a trail of enchantment and wonder in their wake.

Among the indigenous peoples of North America, the Northern Lights were often seen as the celestial form of the great Sky Serpent. According to legend, this immense serpent slithered through the night sky, its vibrant scales casting a radiant glow upon the world below. The serpent's movement across the heavens was believed to represent life's cyclical nature and the Earth's renewal. Its awe-inspiring presence in the night sky was seen as a reminder of the interconnectedness of all living things and the eternal cycle of creation and rebirth.

Ancient Greek mythology attributed the Northern Lights to the goddess Astraea, the divine personification of the stars and the cosmic order. It was said that Astraea, with her golden chariot, traversed the celestial realm, sprinkling stardust and light in her wake. As she glided through the night sky, her radiant presence would manifest as shimmering lights, captivating mortals and igniting their imaginations.

While the Northern Lights are not commonly associated with Celtic mythology, a captivating story from Scotland incorporates these mystical lights. The tale speaks of a legendary Celtic hero named Lugh, who was known for his bravery and cunning.

According to the ancient lore, Lugh embarked on a perilous quest to reach the Land of Eternal Light, a realm rumoured to exist beyond the mortal realm. Guided by ancient druidic knowledge, Lugh ventured into the wild and treacherous Scottish Highlands. As he ascended the mist-shrouded mountains, a blizzard engulfed him, threatening to halt his journey.

In his darkest hour, Lugh called upon the spirits of his ancestors and the ancient gods for guidance. Moved by his sincere plea, the goddess Áine appeared before him, her radiant form emanating ethereal light. She bestowed upon Lugh a magical staff carved from ancient oak and whispered words of power that would guide him through the storm.

As Lugh pressed forward, his staff began to glow with an otherworldly luminescence, illuminating his path through the frozen landscape. The storm clouds above parted, revealing a mesmerising display of shimmering colours in the night sky. The Celtic people believed these lights to be the celestial fire of their ancestors, guiding and protecting Lugh on his quest.

Emboldened by the celestial lights, Lugh journeyed deeper into the heart of the Highlands. He overcame treacherous icy cliffs, crossed roaring rivers, and faced fearsome creatures. With each step, the lights danced and swirled above him, their enchanting display a constant reminder of the divine presence watching over him.

Finally, after days of travel, Lugh reached the edge of the mortal realm and gazed upon the fabled Land of Eternal Light. Its ethereal beauty and vibrant energies were said to be an everlasting source of inspiration and wisdom. Lugh carried the memory of the Northern Lights with him as a symbol of his courageous journey and the connection between the mortal world and the realms beyond.

Though the tale of Lugh and the Northern Lights is not deeply rooted in Celtic mythology, it weaves together elements of Celtic heroes, mystical guidance, and the enchantment of the natural world. It serves as a reminder of the Celtic peoples' reverence for the wonders of the universe and their belief in the interplay between mortal and divine forces.

The story was very different in the south of the border. The lower latitude caused a vantage point where only the top of the aurora was seen. As red was the prominent colour, it was said that the aurora was the reflection of the fallen in a bloody battle to the north. Meanwhile, in Sweden, where life in the coastal regions revolved around the sea, the people always searched for herring. Where there are herring, there are bound to be larger fish. Here, an enchanting tale exists that weaves together the phenomenon of the Northern Lights and the abundant herring populations that grace the waters. This story is known as the Legend of the Herring Flash.

Long ago, in a small fishing village nestled by the shimmering fjords, the people relied on the bountiful herring shoals visiting their shores yearly. The arrival of the herring marked a time of celebration and prosperity, as the silvery fish brought sustenance and abundance to the village.

As the herring migration approached, the village faced an unexpected challenge for one year. A harsh and bitter winter had settled upon the land, freezing the fjords and making it nearly impossible for the herring to reach the village's fishing grounds. The villagers grew worried, for their livelihood and well-being depended on the arrival of the herring.

In the midst of their despair, an elderly fisherman named Gunnar shared an ancient tale passed down through generations. He spoke of a mystical phenomenon called the Herring Flash, said to be a celestial blessing from the gods. According to the legend, during times of great need, the Northern Lights would take on a unique form, shimmering with hues of silver and blue, resembling the very herring the villagers sought.

Inspired by the hope offered by Gunnar's tale, the villagers gathered on the shores, their eyes fixed on the night sky. As darkness descended, a vibrant display of lights emerged. The Northern Lights danced and flickered, painting the heavens with incredible colours. Suddenly, the lights began to transform, swirling and coalescing into the shape of a massive herring shoal.

Filled with awe and wonder, the villagers interpreted the spectacle as a sign. With renewed determination, they set sail, guided by the radiant lights above, which they took as a reflection of an enormous school of herring in the waters beneath. As they cast their nets, the waters teemed with an abundance of herring as if the celestial dance had summoned them forth.

As we now know, the aurora has nothing to do with herring. It's not a bridge, nor is it caused by a fox. The thing these stories have in common is that they don't relate to validation – they relate to answers. These communities throughout history didn't seek validation in their explanation. They sought understanding. Their explanation was woven into the fabric of their lives. We can learn from them. They sought understanding through experience, and we, too, should learn from experience. What we learn translates into our everyday life. We can maximise this by taking every opportunity, hearing every opinion, and learning from the people and the world around us. We aren't here on Earth to close our eyes. We're here to enjoy the ride and to understand the reason why. We're here to get out and experience all the wonders on offer. Through our experiences, we grow, as does our understanding. The most beautiful thing about learning is that nobody can take that knowledge from you.

CHAPTER 17
HYGGE

Comfort, Coziness, Contentment and Wellness

I was exploring a land known for cabin life. As I stepped out of the rental car in the heart of Senja, Norway, after a long drive, a sense of tranquillity washed over me. I sought solace and connection, drawn by the Danish concepts of hygge and Lykke that I had heard so much about. The word itself whispered promises of cosiness, comfort, and the art of savouring life's simplest pleasures. With eager anticipation, armed with my camera, I embarked on a journey that would forever change my perspective.

Segla is often described as Norway in miniature. It's an island in the north, beyond the arctic circle between the Lofoten Islands and Tromsø. Not far away are the ranges where militaries from around the world arrive each winter for their Arctic training. Segla has it all – fjords, mountains, coastlines, tundra- it is a smaller version of Norway as a whole. That day, as the sun began to peek above the horizon, casting a golden glow on the wet peaks, I set my sights on a daring ascent up Mount Segla. The trail unfolded before me, weaving through rocky outcrops and moss-covered terrain. Each step brought me closer to the majestic summit that beckoned me with its awe-inspiring view.

The rugged terrain proved to be both an exhilarating challenge and a humbling reminder of nature's power. With every upward stride, my muscles burned, and my heart pounded with determination. The path grew steeper, demanding careful navigation and unwavering focus. But as the landscape unfolded beneath me, revealing sweeping vistas of the fjords and cascading waterfalls, my weariness dissolved into sheer awe.

The hike demanded not only physical strength but also unwavering mental fortitude. I encountered narrow ledges that clung precariously to the mountainside, requiring utmost concentration and steady nerves. The gusts of wind whipped around me, reminding me of the unpredictable forces of nature. Yet, with each obstacle conquered, I felt a surge of confidence and a profound sense of accomplishment.

With the summit within reach, I pushed forward, the adrenaline fuelling my determination. Finally, as I reached Hesten, the peak with the perfect view of Mount Segla, an awe-inspiring panorama unfolded before my eyes. The vast expanse of Senjas peaks stretched as far as the eye could see, juxtaposed against the tranquil fjords and azure sky. It was a moment of pure triumph, a testament to the resilience of the human spirit and the beauty that awaits those who dare to venture into the unknown.

As I stood there on the summit, I realised that the physical and mental demands of the hike were a metaphor for life itself. It taught me that challenges may arise, testing our limits and pushing us beyond our comfort zones. But through perseverance and a relentless pursuit of our goals, we discover the extraordinary strength that lies within us.

With the view etched in my memory and a renewed sense of purpose, I began my descent, cherishing every step along the trail. The experience of hiking up Segla not only rewarded me with unparalleled views but also instilled in me a profound gratitude for the beauty of nature, the power of resilience, and the immeasurable growth that can be found in the face of adversity. Exhausted, I made my way back.

Through snowy landscapes and frost-kissed forests, I found my way to a secluded wooden cabin nestled amidst towering pines. The air was crisp, and the ground was adorned with a pristine blanket of snow. I entered the cabin, greeted by a crackling fire in the hearth, its warm embrace reaching out to me like an old friend. The pine aroma mingled with the scent of my freshly brewed coffee, an irresistible invitation to unwind and embrace the present moment and the day's success.

As the snowflakes danced outside the window, I wrapped myself in a soft blanket and settled into a plush armchair. The flickering glow of candlelight cast a gentle ambience, casting enchanting shadows across the room. The sound of crackling wood and the soft hum of nature's symphony provided the perfect soundtrack for reflection.

With each sip of coffee, I felt a sense of gratitude for this precious moment of tranquillity. The world outside seemed distant and unimportant as the magic of hygge enveloped my soul. Time slowed down, and worries melted away. In this wooden sanctuary, I discovered the true essence of hygge—a celebration of simplicity, contentment, and the joy of embracing the present.

As evening descended, I ventured outside, the cold winter air kissing my cheeks. The snow beneath my feet whispered stories of serenity, urging me to embrace the enchantment of nature's embrace. I gazed up at the star-studded sky, a vast canvas of wonder. The Northern Lights danced above, their ethereal colours illuminating the night, a reminder of the beauty that lies beyond our grasp.

Returning to the cabin, I cocooned myself in a cosy blanket and lost myself in ideas by the fireside. The crackling flames danced, and my mind transported me to distant lands and wondrous adventures. At this moment, surrounded by the simple pleasures that hygge offers, I realised that true richness lies not in material possessions, but in the moments of connection, warmth, and reflection we create. There's a well-known phrase in travel that goes, 'Take nothing but memories, leave nothing but footsteps.' It was never more true. I travel to collect moments, not things.

I felt a profound sense of peace as I drifted to sleep that night. The concept of hygge had revealed its transformative power. It taught me that amidst the chaos and demands of life, there is deep beauty in finding solace, embracing simplicity, and cherishing the small moments that warm our hearts.

In that wooden cabin, amidst the snow-covered landscape, I was inspired to carry the spirit of hygge with me beyond this serene retreat. Armed with the knowledge that true joy can be found in the simplest of moments, I embarked on a journey to infuse my life with the warmth, connection, and contentment that hygge had bestowed upon me.

CHAPTER 18
CODDIWOMPLE

Travelling Purposefully Towards A Vague Destination

As I stepped out onto the shores of the Faroe Islands, having travelled 1090km by ferry as the crow flies, a sense of adventure coursing through my veins. With each breath of the crisp, salty air, I felt an irresistible call to explore the unique landscapes that lay before me. I had embarked on this journey with no particular destination in mind but a purposeful longing to immerse myself in the beauty of this untamed archipelago. I had a week in Kofifernweh to explore as much as possible before leaving for Seyðisfjörður, Iceland.

The Faroe Islands, nestled between the Norwegian Sea and the North Atlantic Ocean, seemed like nature's masterpiece. The rugged cliffs rose majestically from the depths, their dark basalt formations standing as silent sentinels against the relentless waves. It was as if time itself had carved these islands, shaping them into a tapestry of sheer magnificence.

The beauty of the Faroes lay not only in the grandeur of its landscapes but also in the simplicity of its existence. Setting foot upon these mystical isles, I was drawn to the untamed wilderness beyond the quaint villages and narrow roads. Here, life moved at its own unhurried pace, in complete harmony with nature's rhythm.

With each passing day, I embarked upon a new adventure, guided by the winds and tides. I hiked along ancient trails, tracing the footsteps of generations past, and marvelled at the raw power of the cascading waterfalls that tumbled down the cliffs. The untamed beauty of the Faroe Islands whispered secrets to me, inviting me to contemplate life's more profound mysteries. In these vast expanses of solitude, I found solace. With no predetermined path, I surrendered myself to the whims of chance, allowing the islands to guide me through their labyrinthine landscapes. It was a lesson in letting go, embracing the uncertainty and finding meaning in the journey itself. For it is in the process of discovery that we truly come alive.

I stood atop vertigo-inducing cliffs, where the winds whispered ancient tales in my ear. Every corner of the Faroe Islands held a hidden gem, a secret vista waiting to be unveiled. In the darkness of night, the mystical Northern Lights graced the heavens, painting an ephemeral masterpiece of vibrant colours.

Tórshavn, the capital city, embraces visitors with its captivating blend of old-world allure and modern vibrancy. Nestled along a picturesque harbour, colourful wooden houses line the narrow streets, inviting wanderers to explore its hidden corners. The historic Tinganes district, with its turf-roofed buildings, offers a glimpse into the island's Viking past. At the same time, the bustling harbour buzzes with activity, showcasing the Faroese seafaring heritage.

Embarking on the hike to Bøsdalafossur is like stepping into a magical realm where reality seems to bend. The anticipation builds as you traverse the rugged terrain, surrounded by rolling hills and cliffs. Then, suddenly, an astonishing sight unfolds before your eyes—the optical illusion of Sørvágsvatn, also known as Leitisvatn. This vast freshwater lake appears to defy gravity as it seemingly spills over the edge of the cliffs and merges with the roaring ocean below. The mesmerising interplay of land, water, and the distant horizon creates a surreal experience, challenging your perception of depth and distance. It's a moment that leaves you in awe, contemplating the mysteries of nature and the wonders that can unfold when our senses play tricks on us.

Gasadalur and Múlafossur, nestled on the western coast of the Faroe Islands, form a picturesque duo that captures the essence of the archipelago's beauty. Gasadalur, a charming village perched on the edge of a steep mountainside, offers awe-inspiring vistas of the rugged coastline and the vast expanse of the Atlantic Ocean. Its cluster of colourful houses, adorned with turf roofs, harmonises with the surrounding verdant landscapes, creating a postcard-worthy scene. Just a short hike away lies Múlafossur, a captivating waterfall that cascades from the cliffs into the tumultuous sea below. The sight of Múlafossur is genuinely mesmerising as the roaring water plunges gracefully into the azure waters, creating an enchanting dance of nature's elements. Gasadalur and Múlafossur epitomise the Faroe Islands' spellbinding beauty, inviting visitors to immerse themselves in the untamed wonders of this remote paradise.

Further north, the village of Gjógv emerges as a hidden gem nestled within a stunning fjord. Encircled by towering cliffs, this picturesque settlement offers a serene retreat from the outside world. Wander along the winding footpaths, explore the natural sea-filled gorge after which the village is named, and immerse yourself in the tranquillity of this remote paradise.

Saksun, a hidden gem nestled within the dramatic landscapes of the Faroe Islands, is a place where time seems to stand still. This picturesque village captures the essence of untouched beauty with its remote location and awe-inspiring surroundings. As you approach Saksun, you are greeted by a tranquil fjord snaking its way through lush green valleys guarded by towering mountains. With its cluster of traditional turf-roofed cottages, the village exudes a sense of old-world charm, harking back to a simpler time. Wander through the narrow paths and feel the serenity wash over you as you take in the panoramic vistas. It's a place where the harmony between human habitation and nature is palpable, leaving you with a profound appreciation for the Faroes' natural allure.

In the remote village of Kirkjubøur, history comes alive. As you wander through the village's moss-covered stone houses, you can't help but feel a deep connection to the island's past and the enduring spirit of its people. This ancient settlement, with its atmospheric ruins and well-preserved medieval church, stands as a testament to the Faroes' cultural heritage.

These are just a few glimpses into the tapestry of towns and villages that adorn the Faroe Islands. Each settlement, with its distinct character, beckons travellers to explore its narrow streets, soak in the impressive panoramas, and discover the warmth and hospitality of the Faroese people. Amidst the idyllic landscapes and serene seascapes, these communities offer a true escape from the ordinary, transporting visitors to a realm where time slows down, and the wonders of nature unfold in all their glory.

The Faroe Islands taught me the art of being present, of savouring each moment as it unfolded. This remote haven offered a sanctuary for contemplation and introspection in a world filled with constant noise and distractions. I discovered that purposeful travel was not merely about seeing as much as possible but about seeing with intention, with a mind open to wonder and a heart receptive to the profound beauty of existence. The destination at the end of the road was less important than the journey's intent. In a world that often urges us to plan meticulously, set goals, and follow predefined paths, there exists a concept that challenges conventional wisdom and beckons us to embrace the unknown. Coddiwomple—a verb born out of wanderlust and a thirst for adventure—invites us to embark on a journey with no specific destination in mind, where the purpose lies not in reaching a predetermined end but in the transformative experiences encountered along the way.

Coddiwompling is an invitation to let go of the constraints of control and surrender ourselves to the whims of spontaneity. It is a call to break free from the comfort of routines and venture into uncharted external and internal territories. By wandering without a fixed course, we open ourselves up to serendipitous encounters, unexpected detours, and the sheer magic that unfolds when we allow life to surprise us.

In the Faroe Islands, the emphasis shifted from the destination to the process of exploration itself. I savoured the journey, immersed myself in the present moment, and engaged fully with my surroundings. It was a reminder that life is not a race to be won but a tapestry to be woven, one experience at a time. With each step taken, we gather fragments of wisdom, forge deeper connections with the world and ourselves, and cultivate a profound sense of self-discovery.

Coddiwompling nourishes the spirit of curiosity and the thirst for continuous learning. It encourages us to step outside our comfort zones, seek new perspectives, and embrace the uncertainties that come with venturing into the unfamiliar. Through this intentional embrace of the unknown, we cultivate resilience, adaptability, and a deeper understanding of our strengths and limitations. So, I encourage you to don your explorer's hat, venture forth with an open heart and curious mind, and embark on a coddiwomple of your own. In doing so, you may discover that the true beauty lies not in reaching a predetermined destination but in the extraordinary journey itself.

As I reluctantly bid farewell to these enchanting isles, I carried with me the memories of an unforgettable journey. The Faroe Islands had left an indelible mark upon my soul, a reminder that life's most authentic treasures lie not in the destination but in the transformative power of the journey itself. And as I sailed away, I knew that the Faroe Islands would forever hold a special place in my heart. This eternal flame would ignite my spirit whenever I sought solace in nature's embrace.

CHAPTER 19
RESFEBER

The Relentless Race Of The Travellers Heart Before The Journey Begins

The concept of resfeber was most potent in my heart as I prepared to embark on a motorbike journey from London, UK, to the Atlanterhavsveien (The Atlantic Ocean Road) in Norway. Resfeber is that familiar mix of excitement and apprehension that fills your soul before embarking on a grand adventure. This restlessness ignited my spirit as I straddled my trusty motorbike in London, ready to ride towards the untamed wonders of the Atlantic Ocean Road in Norway. The bike was a Triumph Explorer for those keen on two-wheeled machines. For two weeks, I would traverse vast distances, cross waters, and brave the elements, all in pursuit of the incredible sense of achievement and adventure that awaited me. I was fortunate to have the support of Triumph and Passion Passport for this outrageous adventure, writing pieces for both of them. The entire reason I decided this was a good idea was the fact that this was listed time and again as one of the best driving roads in the world. I've driven many of the roads that make these lists, so I had to add this to my own list.

With the engine humming beneath me, I bid farewell to the familiar streets of Putney, London. I embarked on a quest that would push my limits and expand my horizons. The channel tunnel ferried me beneath the English Channel, connecting two worlds as if symbolising the gateway to the unknown that lay ahead. As I emerged onto the foreign soil of France, a sense of liberation washed over me, and I knew that I had truly begun my odyssey.

Navigating through picturesque landscapes and weaving through winding roads, I crossed borders and ventured deeper into the heart of Europe. The Colorline Super Speed ferry carried me across vast waters, a mere speck amidst the expanse of the North Sea. It was a time of reflection as I stood on the deck, the wind tugging at my clothes, contemplating the immense power and beauty of the ocean beneath.

Norway greeted me with open arms, its snow-kissed mountains and fjords weaving a tapestry of raw natural beauty. The air was crisp, and the scent of pine hung in the wind. Riding through the Norwegian countryside, I felt a profound sense of connection with the land, as if each curve of the road whispered stories of ancient folklore and the resilience of its people.

Approaching Lillehammer, riding past the ski jump used in the 1994 Winter Olympics, a blanket of snow graced the ground, transforming the landscape into more of a challenge. With cautious determination, I continued onwards, relishing the thrill of navigating through the wintry terrain, the bike's tires cutting through the occasional icy crust. It was a sight that took my breath away—a testament to the ever-changing nature of the journey.

The terrain around me transformed from open plains to grand valleys before closing into tight granite gorges as I continued to make tracks. And then, finally, I arrived at the Atlantic Ocean Road, a meandering ribbon of asphalt that danced with the waves of the wild sea. It was a sight to behold—a symphony of engineering marvels and untamed nature. Riding up and down the road, again and again, I felt an indescribable sense of exhilaration. The roaring waves crashed against the rugged shores, the wind whipped through my helmet, and I was immersed in a sensory symphony that ignited my spirit.

The Arctic wind kissed my cheeks, and I revelled in the knowledge that I had conquered fear and doubt, replacing them with a deep-rooted sense of accomplishment. In the depths of those moments, I discovered the true essence of adventure—a fusion of adrenaline and serenity, a dance between the known and the unknown. It was a triumph of the human spirit, of pushing boundaries and embracing the transformative power of the journey.

As I turned back towards London, retracing the miles and memories, I couldn't help but reflect on the resfeber that had sparked this incredible journey. It was the restlessness within that had propelled me forward, the insatiable desire to experience life in all its raw and unfiltered glory. I had answered that call, embarking on a pilgrimage of the soul. I emerged with a heart brimming with gratitude and a mind illuminated by the world's vastness.

This motorbike ride from London to the Atlantic Ocean Road was not merely a physical expedition but a journey of the spirit, an odyssey of self-discovery and natural wanderlust. It revealed to me that the true beauty of life lies not only in reaching the destination but in the transformative power of the journey itself. It taught me that the most remarkable achievements lie beyond our comfort zones and that true fulfilment is found in embracing the unknown and pushing the limits of our own capabilities.

The road back was filled with a mix of emotions—a tinge of sadness to leave the enchanting landscapes behind, yet a profound sense of fulfilment for having experienced something truly extraordinary. The memories etched in my mind, the friendships forged along the way, and the lessons learned would forever remain with me as cherished treasures.

As I rolled back into the bustling streets of London, 5088km later, I couldn't help but marvel at the stark contrast between the two worlds I had traversed—the serene, untouched nature of Norway and the urban chaos of the city. It was a reminder that life is a tapestry woven with diverse experiences, and our willingness to explore and embrace the unknown adds vibrancy to its threads.

Resfeber—the initial restlessness that had set me on this grand adventure—had now transformed into a quiet sense of contentment and wisdom. The road had tested my limits, challenged my fears, and reshaped my perspective. It taught me that the world is vast and teeming with wonders, waiting to be discovered by those with the audacity to chase their dreams.

Looking back at those two weeks, I realised that the true essence of life lies in the pursuit of such moments—

moments of pure exhilaration, moments that make us feel alive. In those moments, we shed the shackles of routine, step outside our comfort zones, and find ourselves genuinely immersed in the present.

So, to all the dreamers and adventurers yearning to embark on their own odyssey, I urge you to embrace the resfeber within you. Whether it be riding through snow-kissed landscapes, crossing vast waters, or conquering unknown paths, let the adventure be a testament to your willingness to embrace the unknown. Listen to the call of the open road, feel the wind in your hair, and let the journey become a testament to your courage and spirit.

Ultimately, it is not the miles travelled but the moments experienced that define us. The stories we gather, the connections we forge, and the incredible sense of achievement that come with pushing beyond our limits make life truly remarkable. So, let the resfeber guide you, ignite your spirit, and take you on a journey that will forever be etched in your heart. Adventure awaits, my fellow travellers—embrace it, relish it, and let it shape you into the fearless soul you were always meant to be. And with that, it's time to address the ultimate question. It's the very title of this book. What is the meaning of life? In the pages of this book, I've told stories of my journey and the lessons I've learned. I've shown that despite whatever appearance is given in the photos I share that convey a sense of perfection, I am flawed, and things often go wrong. We are all imperfect; our life stories are filled with mistakes, wrong turns, heartache, and (hopefully) soaring moments of triumph and joy. The stories in this book come from the stories embedded in the pages of my passport.

At the end of your life, as you reflect upon your journey, you won't be haunted by the ties that kept you bound to safety. You'll realise that the moments that truly defined your existence were born from stepping outside your comfort zone, embracing the unknown, and chasing the sparks of your wildest dreams.

My friend, happiness is an inside job—a power that resides within your heart and spirit. Refuse to grant anyone else the authority to dictate the course of your life. Take hold of the reins and sculpt your own destiny, for you possess the strength to navigate the highs and lows with grace and resilience.

Be the beacon of goodness in a world that sometimes forgets the beauty of humanity. Leave a trail of warmth and light wherever you go, for the impact of your presence can inspire others to believe in the extraordinary power of human connection. Let your actions, kindness, and compassion be why someone believes in the integrity that resides within people's souls.

The chapters of your life are constantly unfolding, and the person you were in the past is not the same as the one you are now. Embrace the growth, the transformations, and the lessons learned. Allow yourself to shed the outdated versions of yourself and embrace the person you have become—a soul brimming with wisdom, resilience, and the audacity to dream.

In this digital age, where Instagram feeds parade the highlight reels of others, it's essential to grant yourself the gift of self-acceptance. The fear of missing out is inconsequential compared to the fear of missing out on embracing your own authenticity. Cut yourself some slack and search within your mind for reasons to be grateful for your unique journey.

Remember, you are worthy of love, respect, and dignity. Even if you lay down for others, they may still find fault in your unwavering support. But that should not diminish your self-worth. Rise above the negativity, stand tall in your truth, and never allow anyone to reduce your inherent value.

Every person you encounter carries a story within them—a tale of triumphs, trials, and the unspoken battles they fight. Therefore, be kind, my dear friend. For within the simplicity of kindness lies the power to heal, uplift, and make a profound difference in someone's life. A gentle smile, a helping hand, or a simple word of encouragement can weave threads of hope into the tapestry of another's existence.

Take pride in your resilient heart, which has endured pain, betrayal, and hardships yet still beats with unwavering strength. It is a testament to your capacity for resilience, forgiveness, and the indomitable spirit that resides within you. Your heart is a beacon of love, ready to share its light with the world.

Now is the time to shed the paradoxes that bind you. Embrace the person you have always aspired to be. Take control of your narrative, for you have the power to rewrite your own story. Embrace happiness with intention, for you deserve a life illuminated by joy, purpose, and fulfilment. Be the change you seek; transformation begins with the conscious decision to step into your authentic self.

Remember, dear soul, you have been granted a single precious existence—a life to be lived fully, embracing awe-inspiring moments, connecting with extraordinary souls, and leaving a trail of kindness and compassion in your wake. Be mindful of the blessings surrounding you, soak in the world's beauty, and relish the simple pleasures that make life truly remarkable.

Engage with the world around you—share conversations with strangers, immerse yourself in the literature that ignites your soul, and let your curiosity lead you to uncharted territories. Choose authenticity over conformity, lend a helping hand to those in need, and find solace in self-care. Pause and breathe in the magic of a sunrise, capturing its fleeting beauty with your heart and lens. Treasure the bonds of friendship, for they are the threads that weave a tapestry of love and support.

Release the chains of negativity and limiting beliefs, for they only confine your spirit. Embrace the exhilaration of facing your fears head-on, for you discover the depths of your courage and resilience within those moments of discomfort. Take leaps of faith and savour the taste of uncertainty, for it is through daring leaps that you uncover hidden facets of your own strength.

As you walk this journey, always remember that the power of empathy and compassion lies in acknowledging that each person you encounter carries their own battles and triumphs. Choose kindness as your compass, for in a world that often feels fragmented, it is kindness that has the power to bind us together, heal wounds, and restore faith in the inherent goodness of humanity.

Revel in the magnificent imperfections of your own story, for it is through vulnerability and self-acceptance that you find the true essence of your being. Embrace the lessons learned from the chapters you cannot rewrite, and with courage, start where you are now to shape a new ending—one that is filled with growth, love, and the pursuit of your dreams.

You are the author of your own narrative. Within your hands lies the power to craft a life that brims with adventure, purpose, and an unwavering belief in the limitless potential that resides within you. So, my dear friend, as you reach the final pages of this chapter, may your heart be filled with gratitude for the resilience that carried you through the storms, for the moments of pure bliss that took your breath away, and for the lessons etched upon your soul.

When people show you who they truly are, believe them. Surround yourself with those who uplift your spirit, celebrate your victories, and stand by you through the trials of life. In choosing the company of those who cherish and support you, you create a symphony of love and encouragement that reverberates through your every step. Your journey is a masterpiece in progress.

And so, my friend, as you turn the final page of this chapter and prepare to embark on the next, remember that your story is far from over. Embrace the uncharted territories, dance with the unknown, and let the echoes of your laughter and resilience resound through the tapestry of your existence. You have the power to shape your destiny, to infuse your life with purpose and passion, and to leave an indelible mark upon the world.

May your journey be filled with unwavering faith, unbreakable courage, and an unyielding belief in the extraordinary magic that lies within you. Embrace the profound truth that you are the architect of your happiness, the guardian of your dreams, and the hero of your own tale.

So go forth, my friend, and let the final words of this chapter be a resounding declaration of your unwavering spirit, unshakable resilience, and unyielding commitment to living a life that is both extraordinary and true to your heart.

As the journey continues, and within you lies the power to create a magnificent symphony of joy, love, and purpose, remember this:

The meaning of life is to give your life meaning.

Printed in Great Britain
by Amazon